# 2026
중등영어 교사임용

# 권영주 임용 전공
# 영어 교육론

MIND MAP

# 영어교육론 MIND MAP 목차 — CONTENS

## 00. 기출분석편

- 01  2언어습득 ··· 009
- 02  교재론 ··· 010
- 03  영어평가 ··· 011
- 04  영어교수법 ··· 012
- 05  듣기지도 ··· 013
- 06  말하기지도 ··· 014
- 07  읽기지도 ··· 015
- 08  쓰기지도 ··· 016
- 09  문법지도 ··· 017
- 10  어휘지도 ··· 018

## 01. Second Language Acquisition

- 01  2언어습득 ··· 021
- 02  행동주의 ··· 022
- 03  인지주의 ··· 023
- 04  선천주의 ··· 024
- 05  정보처리 ··· 025
- 06  사회적 구성주의 (1) ··· 026
- 07  사회적 구성주의 (2) ··· 027

## 02. Learning Principles

- 01  학습 원리 ··· 031
- 02  학습 스타일 ··· 032
- 03  학습 전략 ··· 033
- 04  의사소통 전략 ··· 034
- 05  정의적 측면 ··· 035
- 06  언어학습의 Agency ··· 036

# 영어교육론 MIND MAP 목차 _____ CONTENS

## 03. Communicative Competence

| 01 | 의사소통 능력 | ⋯ 039 |
| 02 | 사회문화적 교수법 | ⋯ 040 |
| 03 | 화용론 | ⋯ 041 |
| 04 | 의미 협상 | ⋯ 042 |
| 05 | 외국인을 위한 화법 | ⋯ 043 |
| 06 | 학습자 언어 | ⋯ 044 |
| 07 | 오류 분석 | ⋯ 045 |
| 08 | 피드백 | ⋯ 046 |
| 09 | Uptake | ⋯ 047 |
| 10 | 증거 | ⋯ 048 |

## 04. Language Teaching Methodology

| 01 | 언어학습 교수법 | ⋯ 051 |
| 02 | 교수 요목 | ⋯ 052 |
| 03 | 전통적 교수법 | ⋯ 053 |
| 04 | 디자이너 교수법 | ⋯ 054 |
| 05 | 의사소통 교수법 | ⋯ 055 |
| 06 | 의사소통 활동 | ⋯ 056 |
| 07 | 과업중심 교수법 (1) | ⋯ 057 |
| 08 | 과업중심 교수법 (2) | ⋯ 058 |
| 09 | 과업중심 교수법 (3) | ⋯ 059 |
| 10 | 내용중심 교수법 | ⋯ 060 |
| 11 | 참여언어 교수법 | ⋯ 061 |
| 12 | 경험언어 교수법 | ⋯ 062 |
| 13 | 어휘중심 교수법 | ⋯ 063 |
| 14 | Focus on Form | ⋯ 064 |

# 영어교육론 MIND MAP 목차 _____ CONTENS

## 05. English Assessment

- 01  언어 평가 ... 067
- 02  평가 원리 (1) ... 068
- 03  평가 원리 (2) ... 069
- 04  시험 유형 (1) ... 070
- 05  시험 유형 (2) ... 071
- 06  대체 평가 (1) ... 072
- 07  대체 평가 (2) ... 073
- 08  시험항목 분석 ... 074

## 06. Teaching Listening

- 01  듣기 지도 ... 077
- 02  듣기 언어의 기능 ... 078
- 03  듣기 자료 ... 079
- 04  듣기 수업형식 ... 080
- 05  듣기 전략 ... 081
- 06  대화체 특성 ... 082
- 07  듣기 활동 ... 083

## 07. Teaching Speaking

- 01  말하기지도 ... 087
- 02  유창성, 정확성, 복합성 ... 088
- 03  말하기 특성 ... 089
- 04  대화말하기 지도 ... 090
- 05  대화제 기제 ... 091
- 06  말하기 과업 ... 092
- 07  말하기 활동 (1) ... 093
- 08  말하기 활동 (2) ... 094

## 08. Teaching Reading

- 01  읽기 지도 ... 097
- 02  읽기수업 과정 ... 098
- 03  읽기 유형 ... 099
- 04  읽기 활동 방법 (1) ... 100
- 05  읽기 활동 방법 (2) ... 101

# 영어교육론 MIND MAP 목차 _____ CONTENS

## 09. Teaching Writing

| 01 | 쓰기 지도 | ⋯ 105 |
| 02 | 과정중심 쓰기 (1) | ⋯ 106 |
| 03 | 과정중심 쓰기 (2) | ⋯ 107 |
| 04 | Genre중심 쓰기 | ⋯ 108 |

## 10. Teaching Grammar

| 01 | 문법 교실 수업 | ⋯ 111 |
| 02 | Focus on Form | ⋯ 112 |
| 03 | 명시적 문법수업 | ⋯ 113 |
| 04 | 문법 교수법 | ⋯ 114 |

## 11. Teaching Vocabulary

| 01 | 어휘 지도 | ⋯ 117 |
| 02 | 어휘 교수법 | ⋯ 118 |
| 03 | Lexis | ⋯ 119 |
| 04 | 어휘 활동 방법 (1) | ⋯ 120 |
| 05 | 어휘 활동 방법 (2) | ⋯ 121 |
| 06 | 발음지도교수법 | ⋯ 122 |
| 07 | 발음 지도 목표 | ⋯ 123 |

권영주 영어교육론 MIND MAP

# 00.
# 기출 분석편

**MEMO**

# 01 2언어 습득

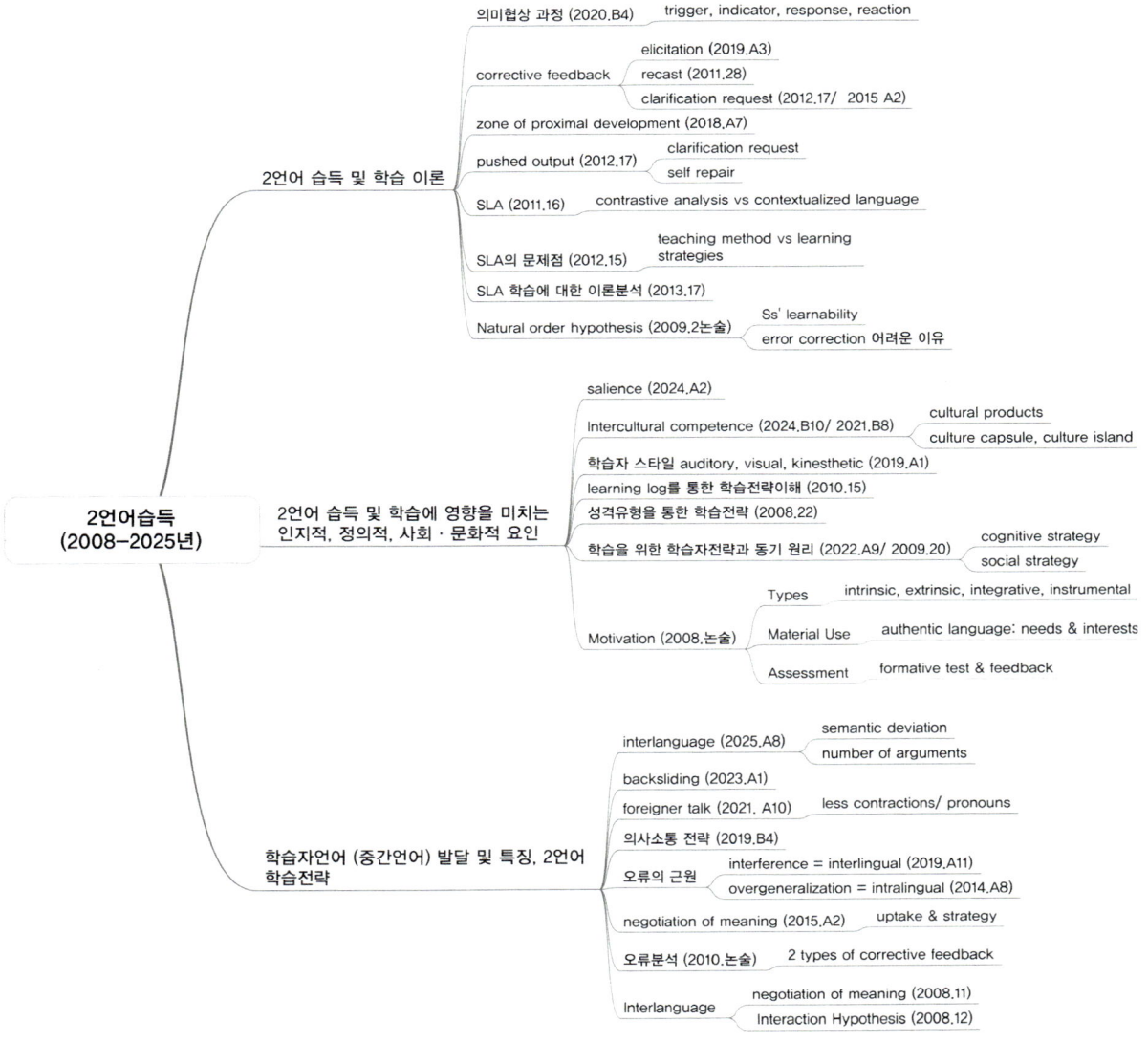

# 02 교재론

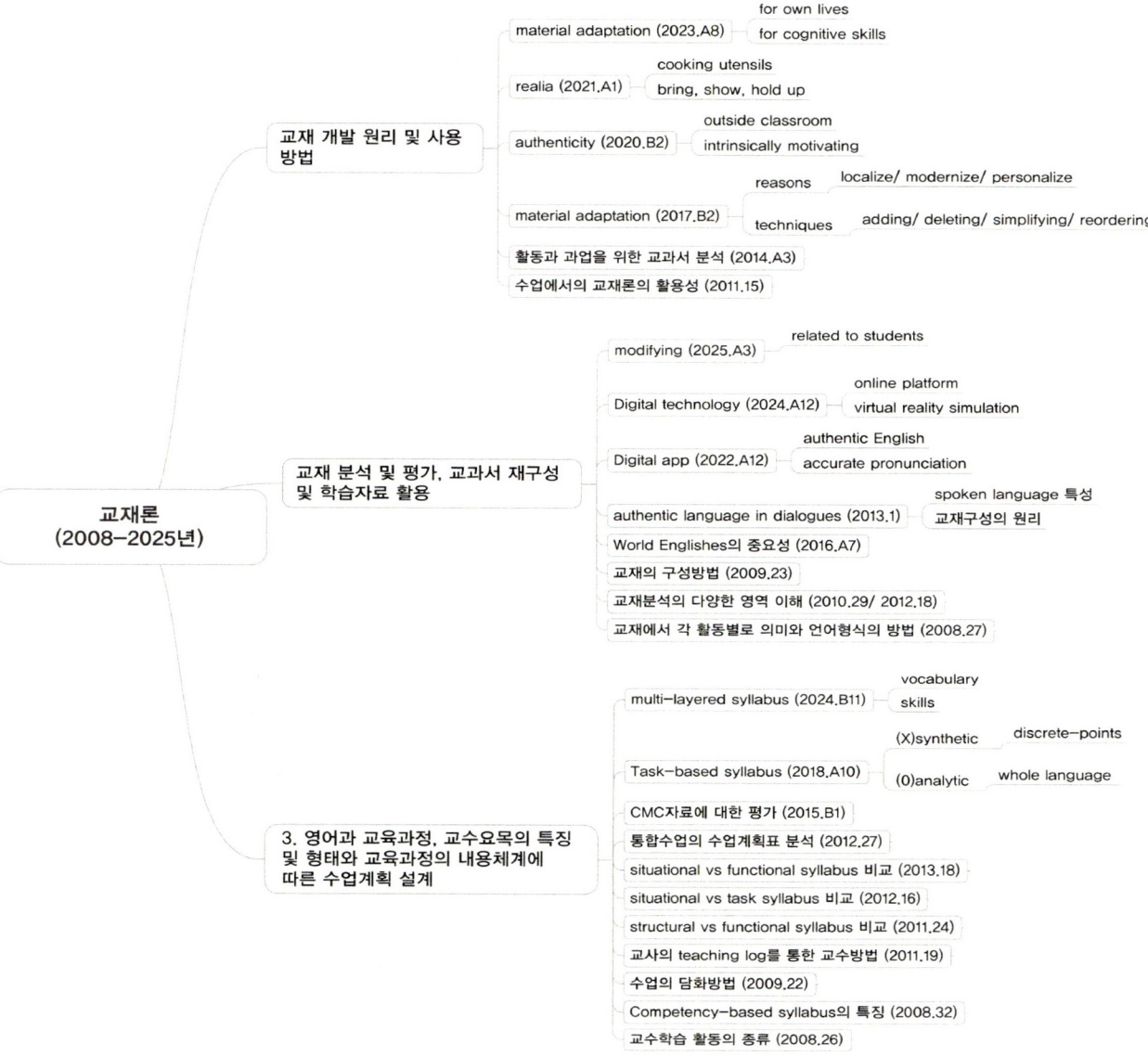

# 03 영어평가

**권영주 영어교육론 MIND MAP**

영어평가 (2008-2025년)
- 영어평가의 기본개념과 원리, 평가 유형
  - Principles
    - practicality (2024.A1)
    - washback (2022.A1)
    - reliability
      - internal consistency (2020.B6)
      - inter-rater reliability (2025.A4/2021.B1/ 2014.A7)
      - intra-rater reliability
    - validity, reliability, washback, authenticity 장단점 (2016.B1)
  - Validity 분석
    - predictive validity (2017.A9)
    - concurrent validity (2020.B6)
    - validity 종류 (2008.20)
    - construct validity (2012.논술) — rating on fluency & cohesion
  - 말하기 평가 (2025.A9)
    - clarity
    - authenticity

- 평가 목적에 부합하는 영어 평가 과업 설계
  - Item analysis (2024.B6)
    - internal consistency
    - concurrent validity
  - Computer adaptive testing (2023.A4)
  - Selected-response items (2023.B11)
    - stem & options: simple and direct
    - a single clearly formulated problem
  - Task types (2021.B9)
    - information transfer
    - partial dictation
  - Assessment Notes (2022.B10)
    - simple sentences
    - story construction
  - Assessment form (2020.B10)
    - language — appropriateness
    - delivery — self-confidence
  - Aptitude test (2019.A12)
    - before beginning language study
    - to place Ss in sections appropriate to their ability
  - Cloze 유형
    - random/ rational-deletion/ C-test (2019.A3)
    - Cloze Test와 C-Test 원리 (2010.21)
  - Holistic/ Analytic scoring
    - 특성비교 (2019.A12)
    - analytic scoring (2012.22) — task/ fluency/ intelligibility
  - Diagnostic test의 특성 (2018.A13)
  - Criterion-/ Norm-referenced test (2012.19)
  - Alternative assessment의 종류 portfolios (2017.A1)
  - Summative vs Formative assessment (2016.B1)
  - 읽기수업에서 self-assessment 분석 (2013.17)
  - Item discrimination & distractors (2015.A3)
  - Multiple choice시험 제작시 유의점 (2013.25)
  - Conferencing을 통한 쓰기 평가 (2010.16)
  - Multiple choice시험에서 항목분석표 이해 (2009.18/2011.21)

# 04 영어교수법

권영주 영어교육론 MIND MAP

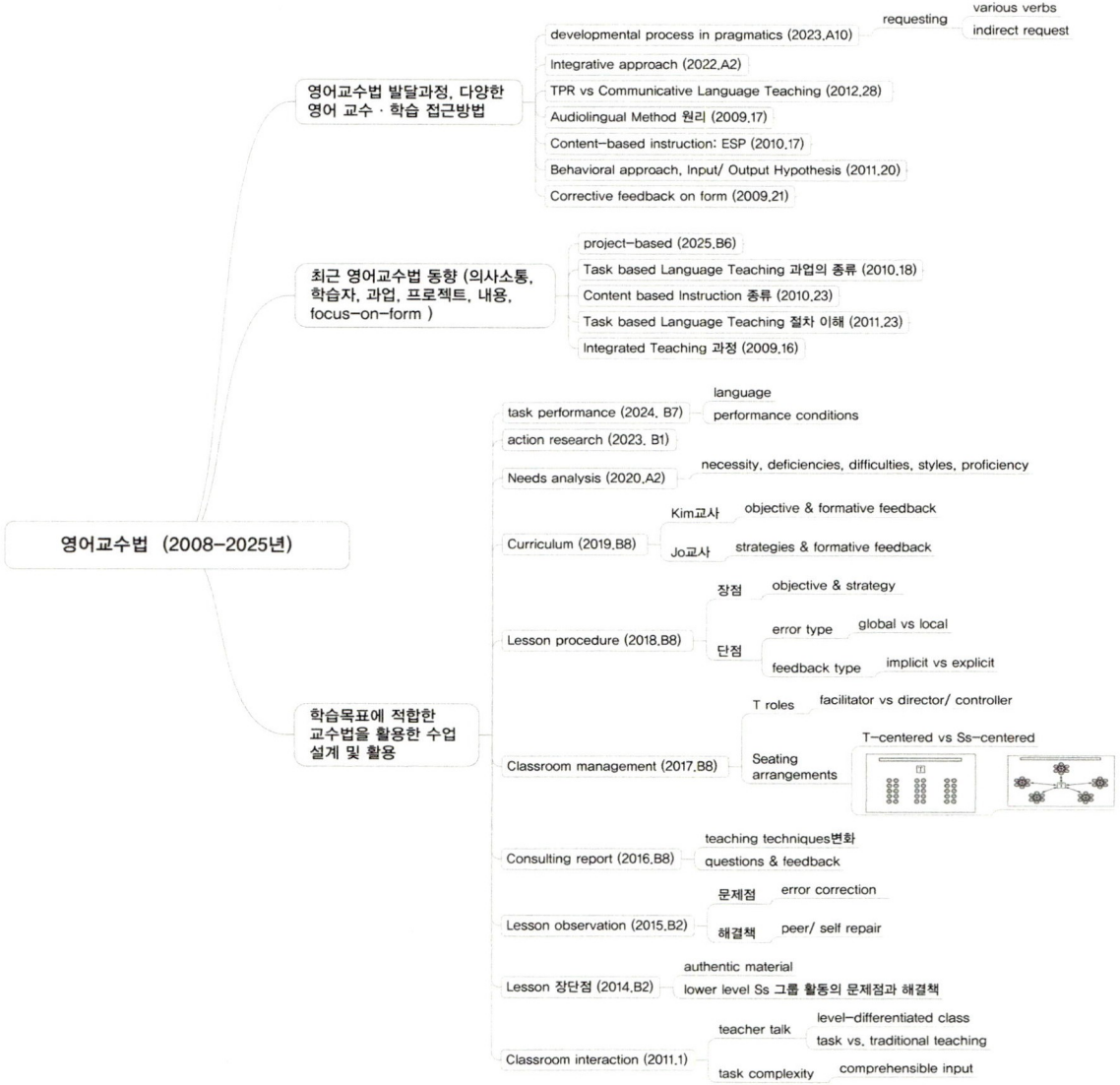

12

# 05 듣기지도

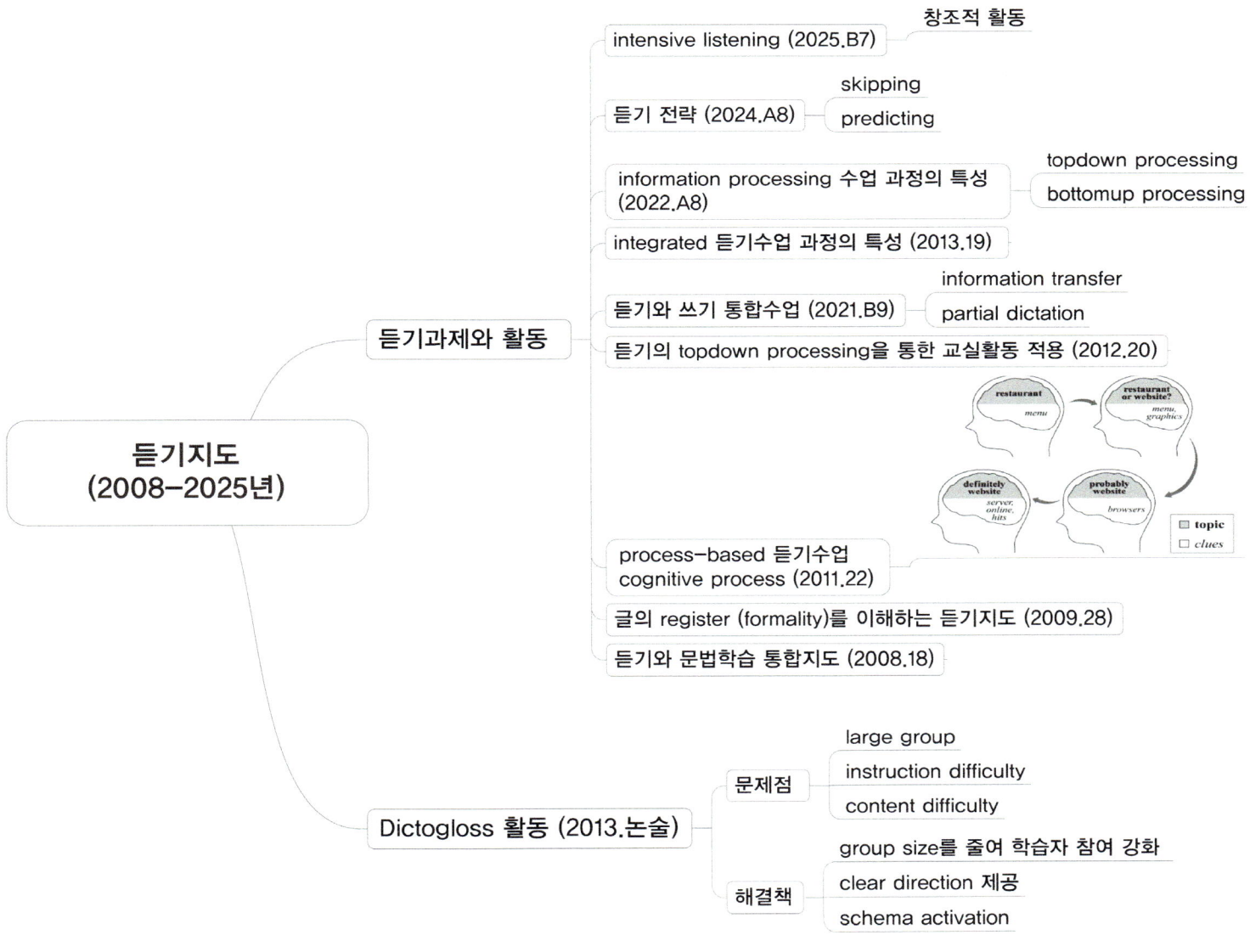

# 06 말하기지도

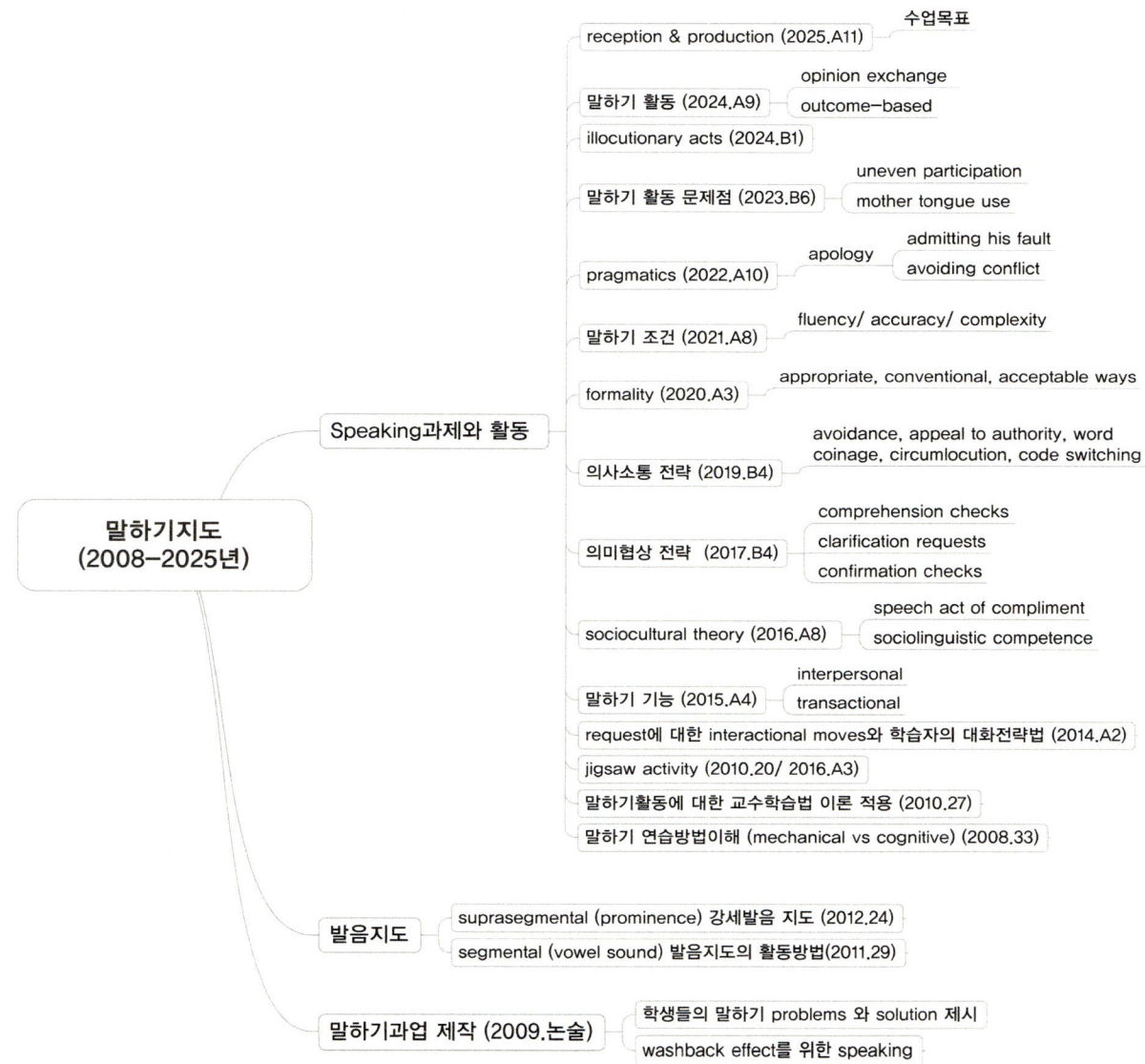

# 07 읽기지도

## 읽기지도 (2008-2025년)

### Reading과제와 활동

- 읽기 전략 (2025.B9) — 문제점과 읽기 전략 제시
- reading activity (2023.A9)
  - word master
  - graphic organizer
- achievement standards (2021.A9)
- outlining technique & summary (2020.A10)
- 읽기전략: skimming & scanning (2017.A6)
- phonics (decoding) approach 문제점 분석 (2017.A13)
- extensive reading (2015.A5)
- 읽기전략: inferencing (2014.A10)
- 읽기수업의 교수접근방법 (2012.26)
- webquest활동을 통한 inquiry-based learning (2011.27)
- 읽기의 pre-, while, post-활동의 절차 (2011.17)

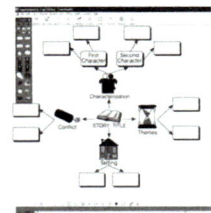

- hypertext의 post-reading 활동 (2009.15)
- bottomup과 topdown을 활용하는 읽기전략 (2008.23)

### Pre-While-Post reading 활동 제작 (2008논술)

- pre-reading
  - motivation
  - vocabulary warmup
  - prediction
- while-reading
  - comprehension
  - skimming & scanning & inferencing
- post-reading
  - confirmation comprehension
  - follow ups

# 08 쓰기지도

# 09 문법지도

권영주 영어교육론 MIND MAP

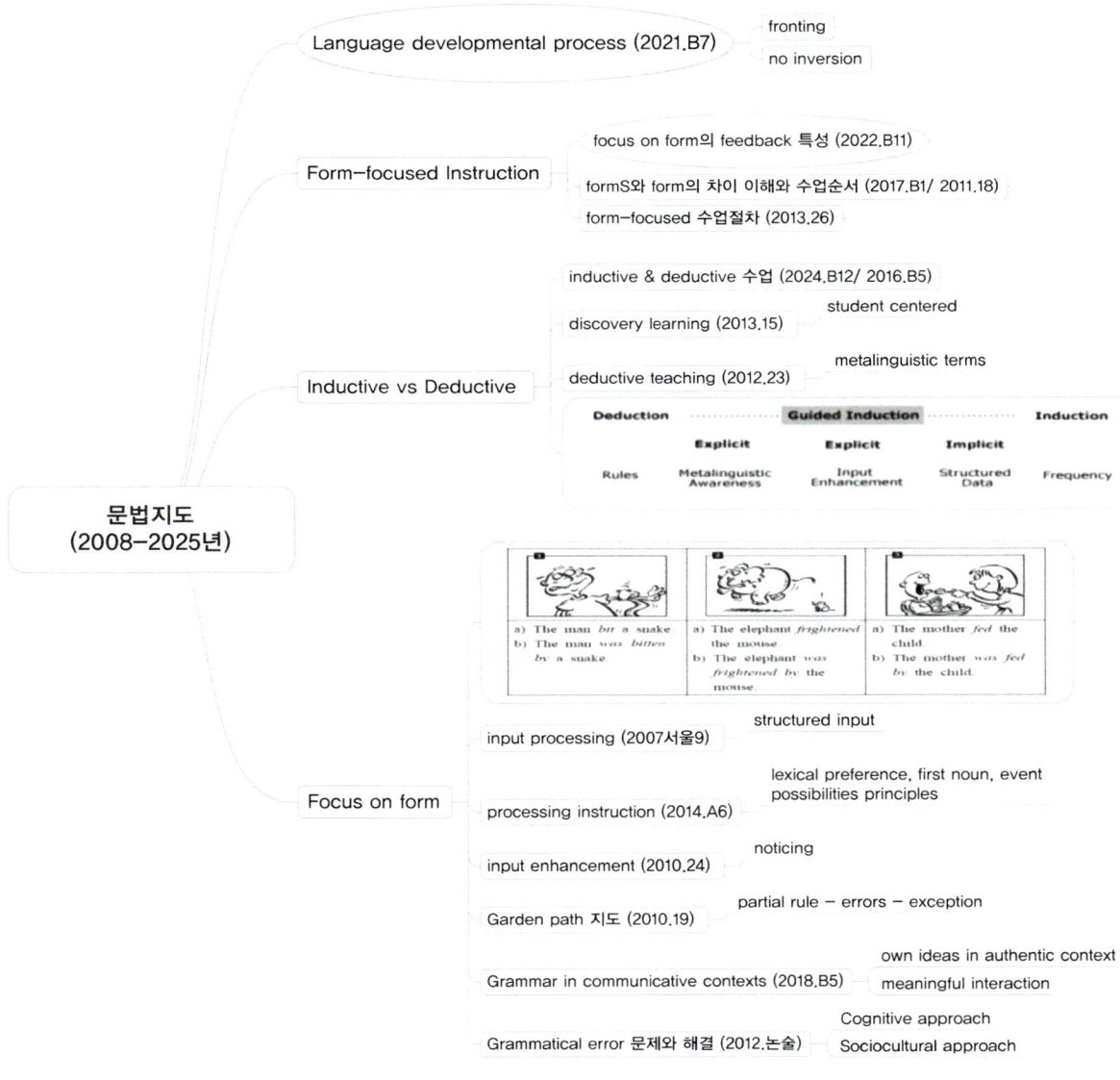

문법지도 (2008-2025년)

- Language developmental process (2021.B7)
  - fronting
  - no inversion

- Form-focused Instruction
  - focus on form의 feedback 특성 (2022.B11)
  - formS와 form의 차이 이해와 수업순서 (2017.B1/ 2011.18)
  - form-focused 수업절차 (2013.26)

- Inductive vs Deductive
  - inductive & deductive 수업 (2024.B12/ 2016.B5)
  - discovery learning (2013.15) — student centered
  - deductive teaching (2012.23) — metalinguistic terms

- Focus on form
  - input processing (2007서울9) — structured input
  - processing instruction (2014.A6) — lexical preference, first noun, event possibilities principles
  - input enhancement (2010.24) — noticing
  - Garden path 지도 (2010.19) — partial rule – errors – exception
  - Grammar in communicative contexts (2018.B5)
    - own ideas in authentic context
    - meaningful interaction
  - Grammatical error 문제와 해결 (2012.논술)
    - Cognitive approach
    - Sociocultural approach

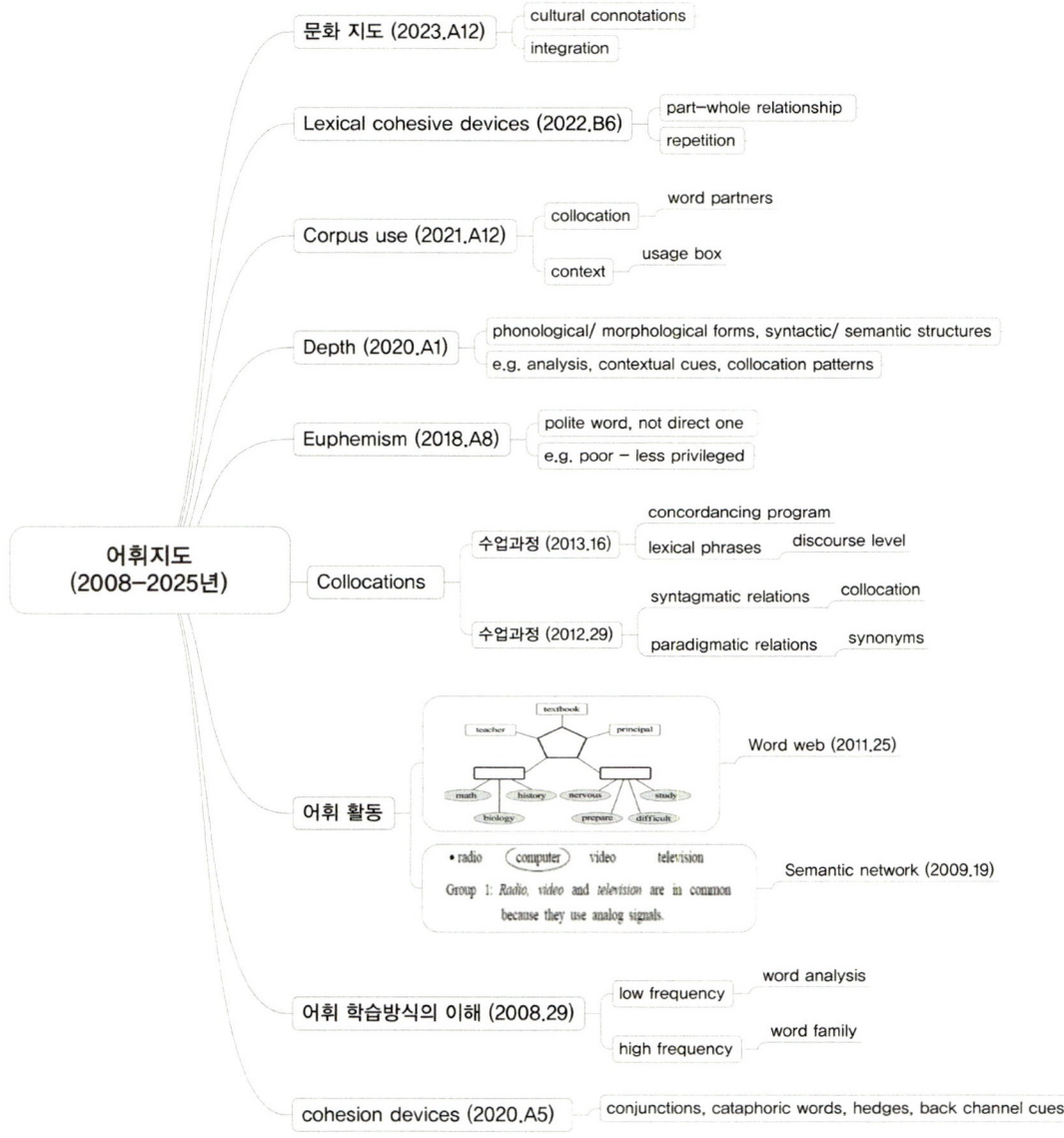

권영주 영어교육론 MIND MAP

# 01.
# Second Language Acquisition

MEMO

# 01 2언어습득

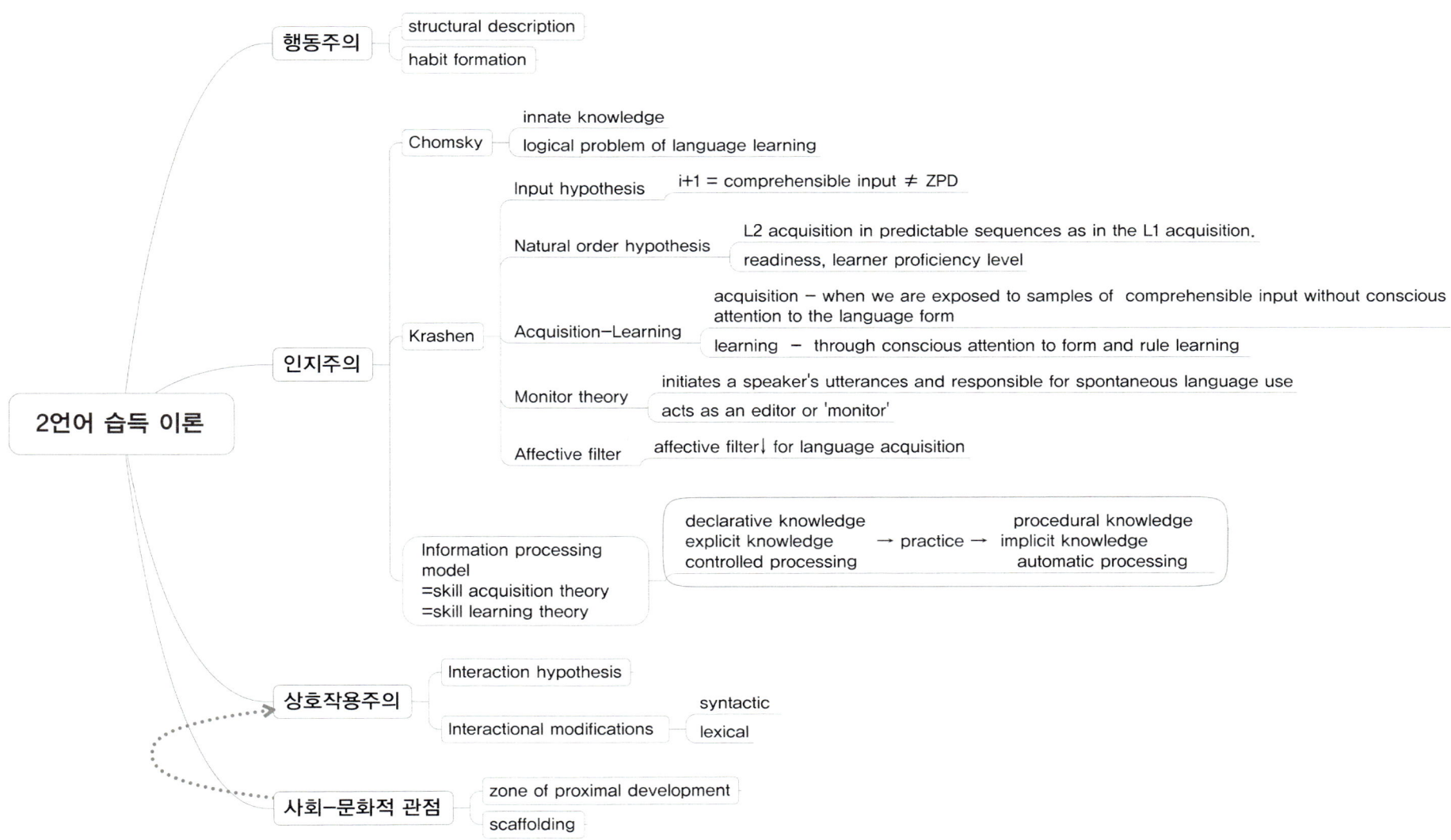

# 02 행동주의

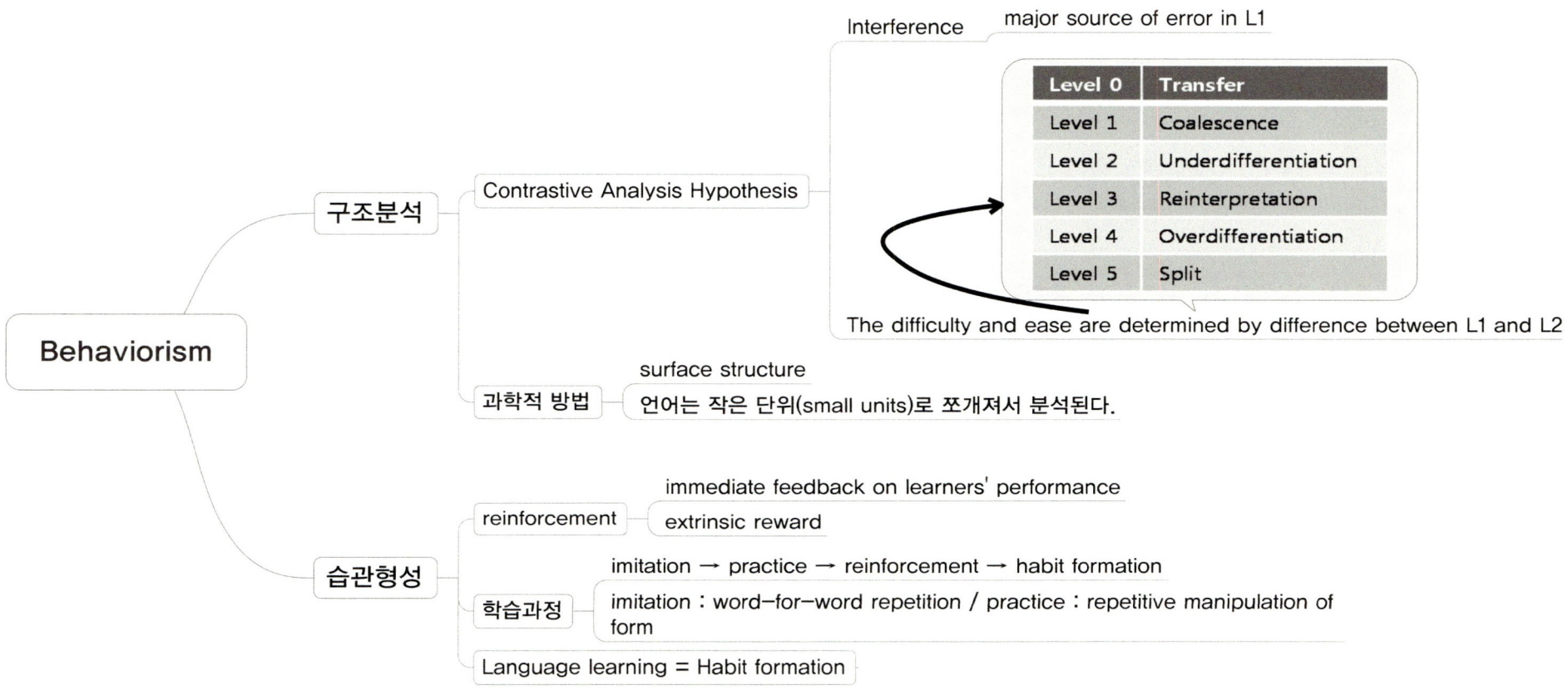

## 03 인지주의

**Cognitivism**

- **Attention-Processing model**
  - focal – peripheral attention
    - focal: 언어에 주의를 기울이고, 의식적으로 언어를 사용하는 학습자로서 이때 사용한 언어는 단기 기억 장치에 보관된다.
    - peripheral: 의사소통에서 언어수행
    - 예) free writes, rapid reading, open-ended group work
  - controlled – automatic processing
    - controlled: explicit & declarative knowledge
    - automatic: implicit & procedural knowledge

- **Implicit – Explicit models**
  - implicit linguistic knowledge — 자동적, 자발적 언어 사용
  - explicit linguistic knowledge — 문법적 지식

|  | IMPLICIT KNOWLEDGE | EXPLICIT KNOWLEDGE |
|---|---|---|
| Memory | Procedural | Declarative |
| Kind of awareness | Intuitive/unconscious | Conscious |
| Access | Available through automatic processing | Available only through controlled processing |
| Evidence | It's reasoning cannot be verbalized | Can be verbalized and explained |

*01 Second Language Acquisition*

## 04 선천주의

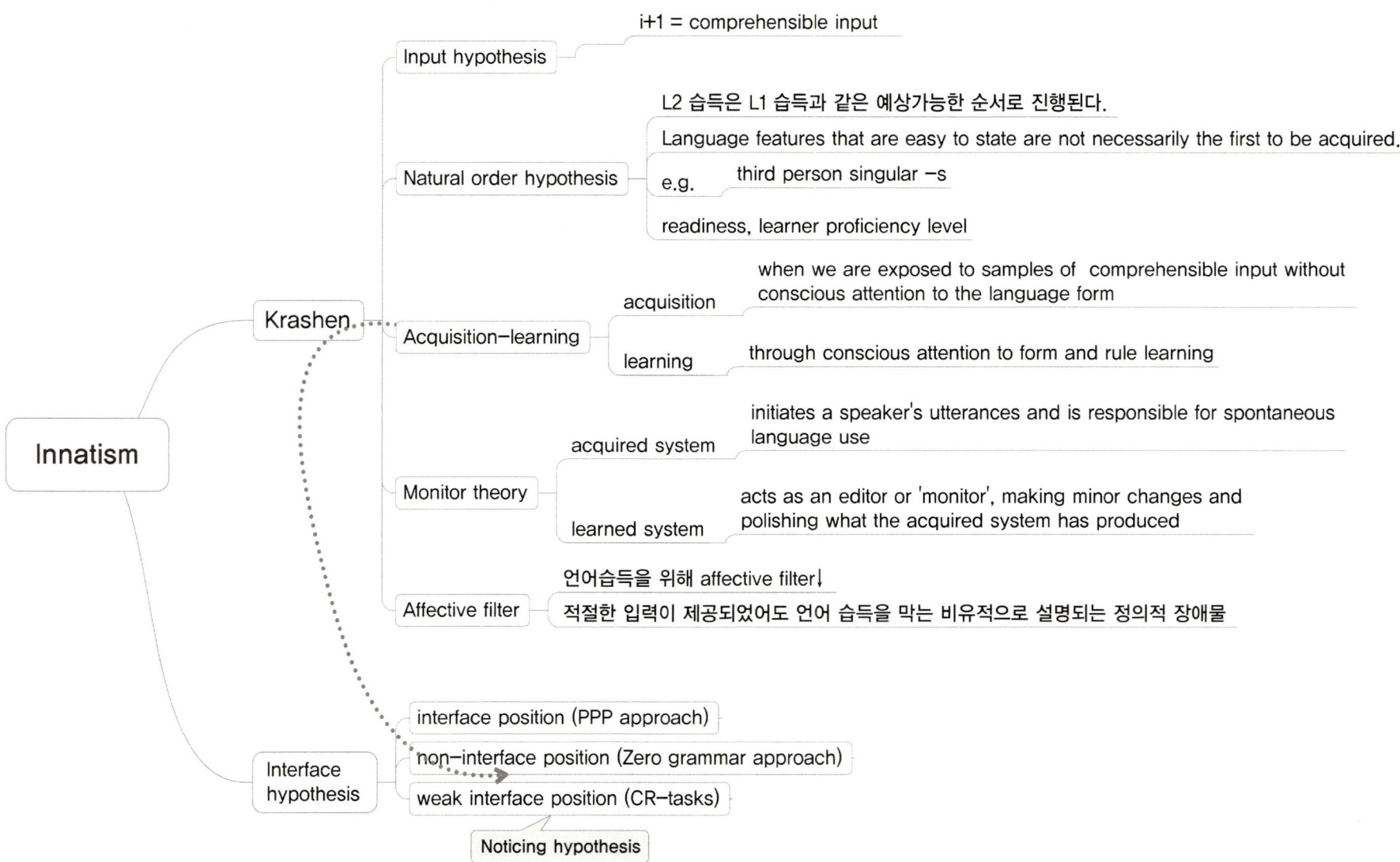

# 05 정보처리

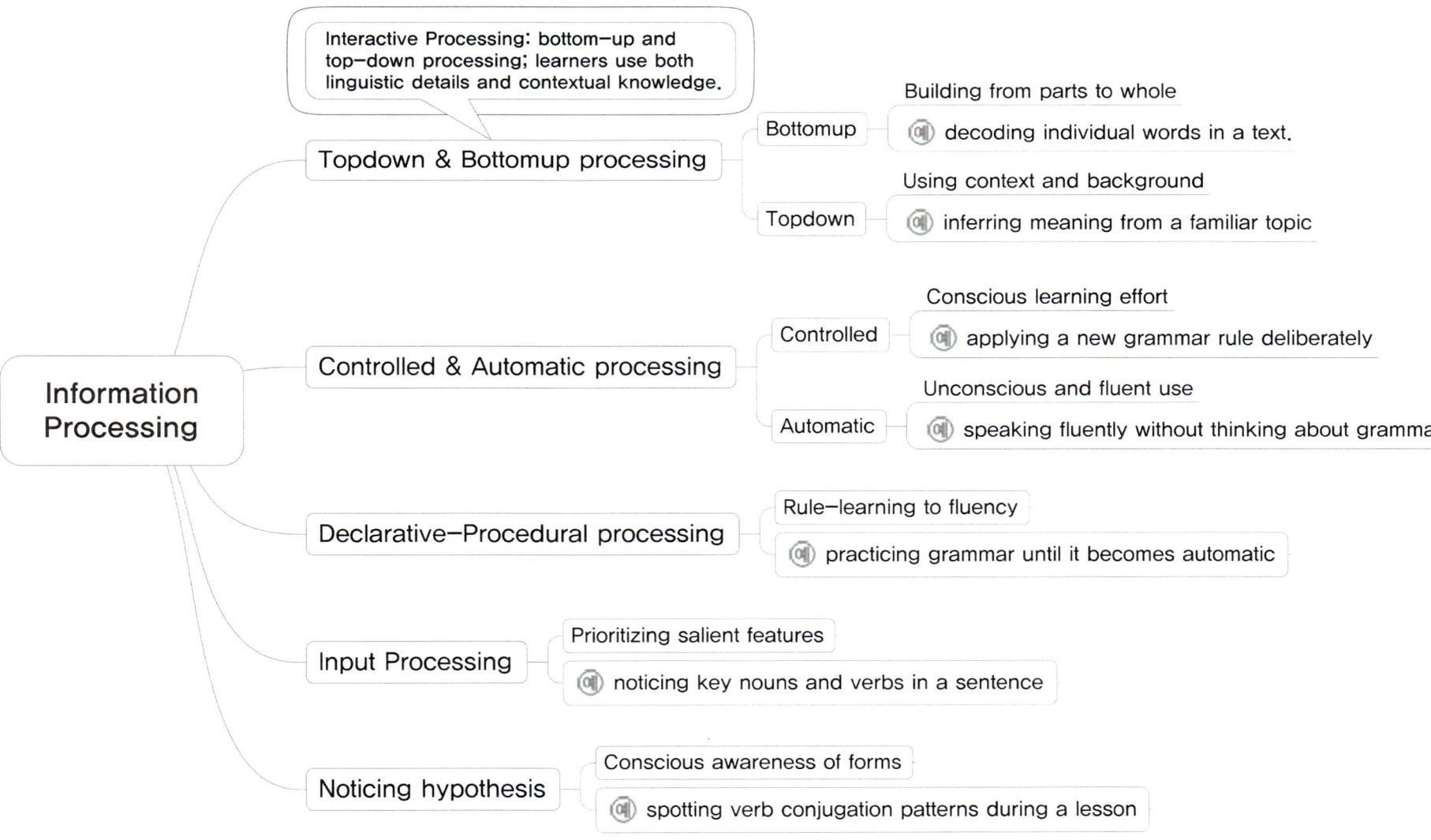

# 06 사회적 구성주의 (1)

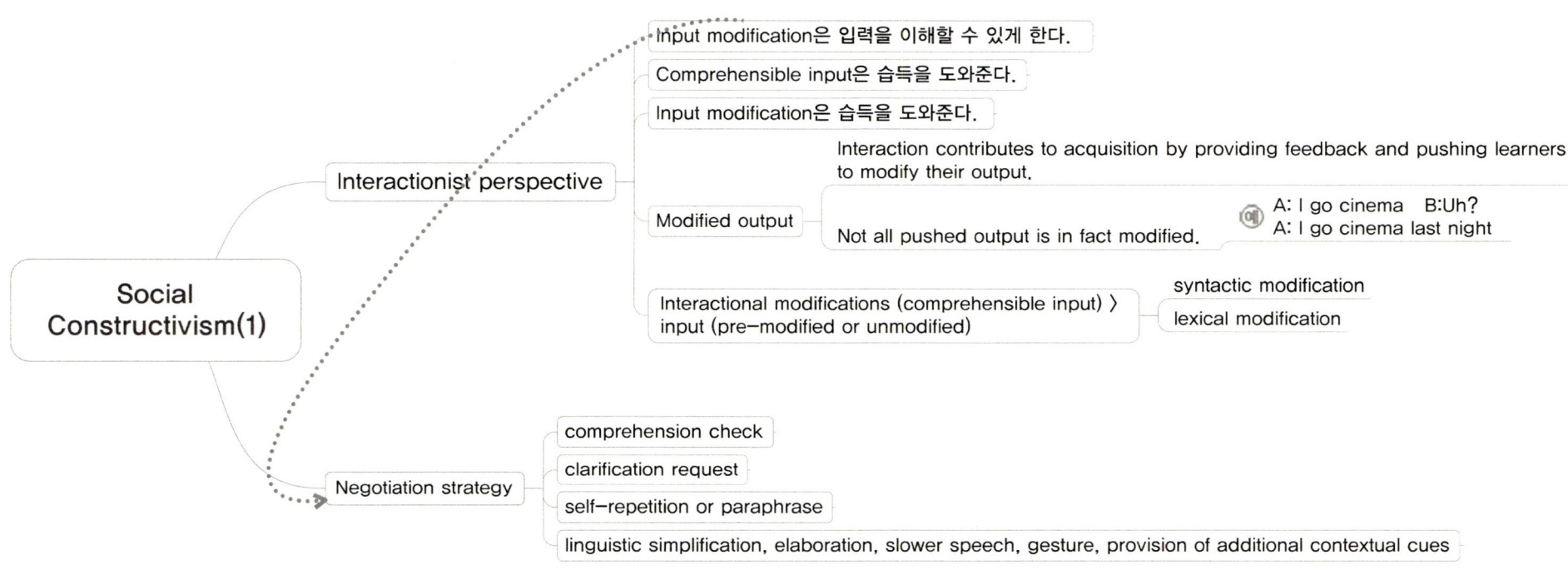

# 07 사회적 구성주의 (2)

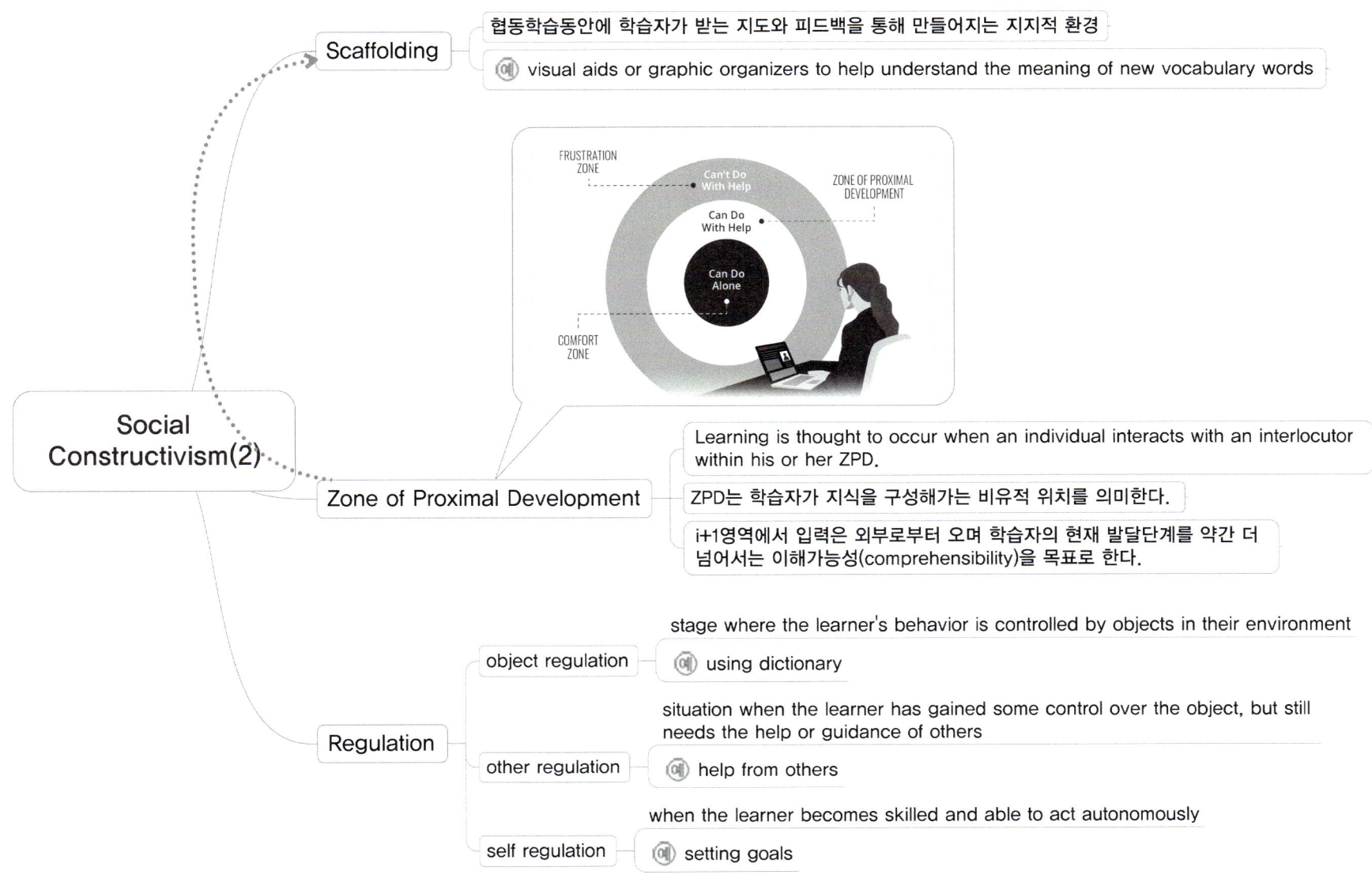

**Social Constructivism(2)**

- **Scaffolding**
  - 협동학습동안에 학습자가 받는 지도와 피드백을 통해 만들어지는 지지적 환경
  - 예) visual aids or graphic organizers to help understand the meaning of new vocabulary words

- **Zone of Proximal Development**
  - Learning is thought to occur when an individual interacts with an interlocutor within his or her ZPD.
  - ZPD는 학습자가 지식을 구성해가는 비유적 위치를 의미한다.
  - i+1영역에서 입력은 외부로부터 오며 학습자의 현재 발달단계를 약간 더 넘어서는 이해가능성(comprehensibility)을 목표로 한다.

- **Regulation**
  - object regulation — stage where the learner's behavior is controlled by objects in their environment
    - 예) using dictionary
  - other regulation — situation when the learner has gained some control over the object, but still needs the help or guidance of others
    - 예) help from others
  - self regulation — when the learner becomes skilled and able to act autonomously
    - 예) setting goals

MEMO

# 02.
## Learning Principles

권영주 영어교육론 MIND MAP

MEMO

# 01 학습 원리

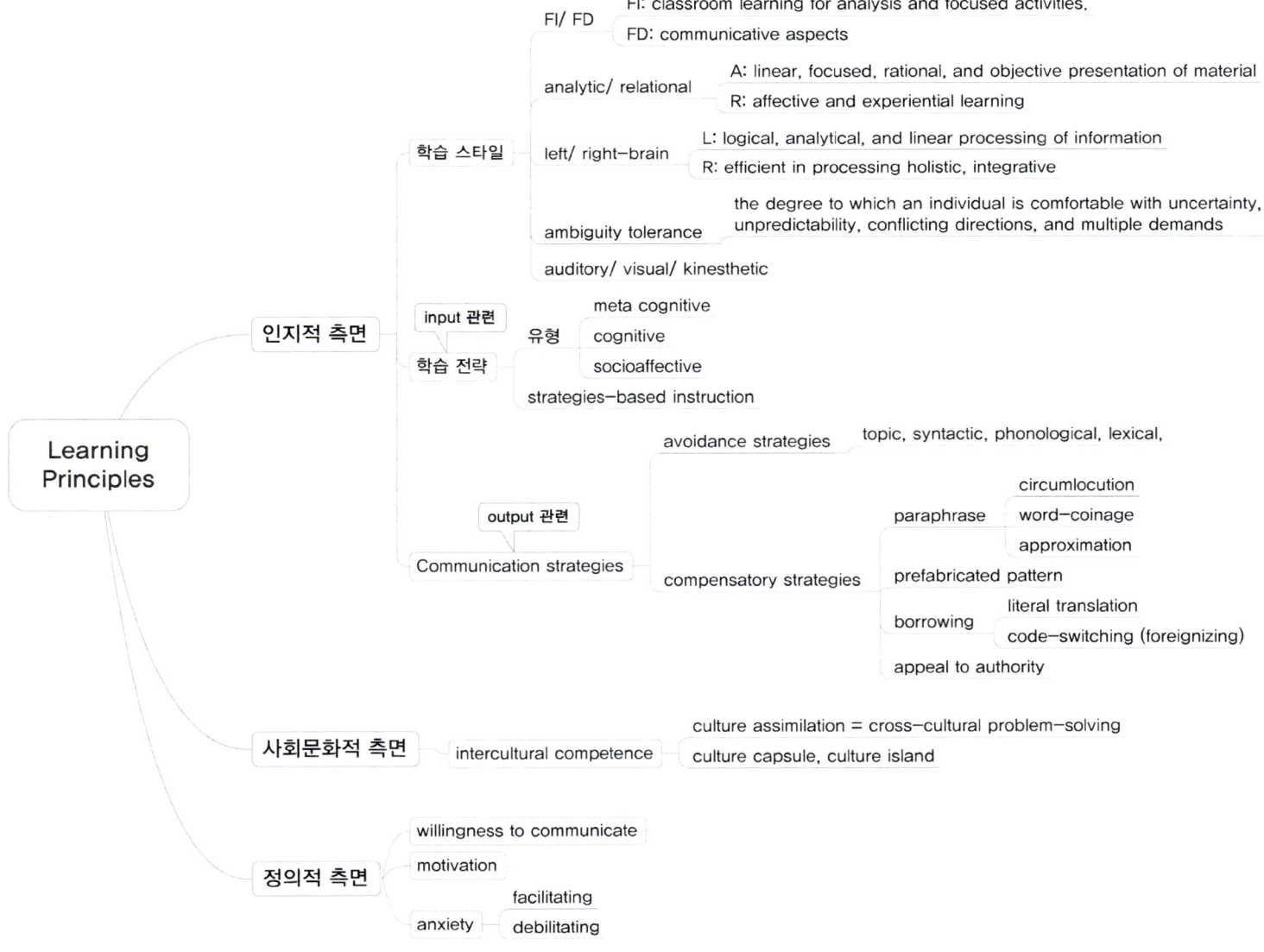

## 02 학습 스타일

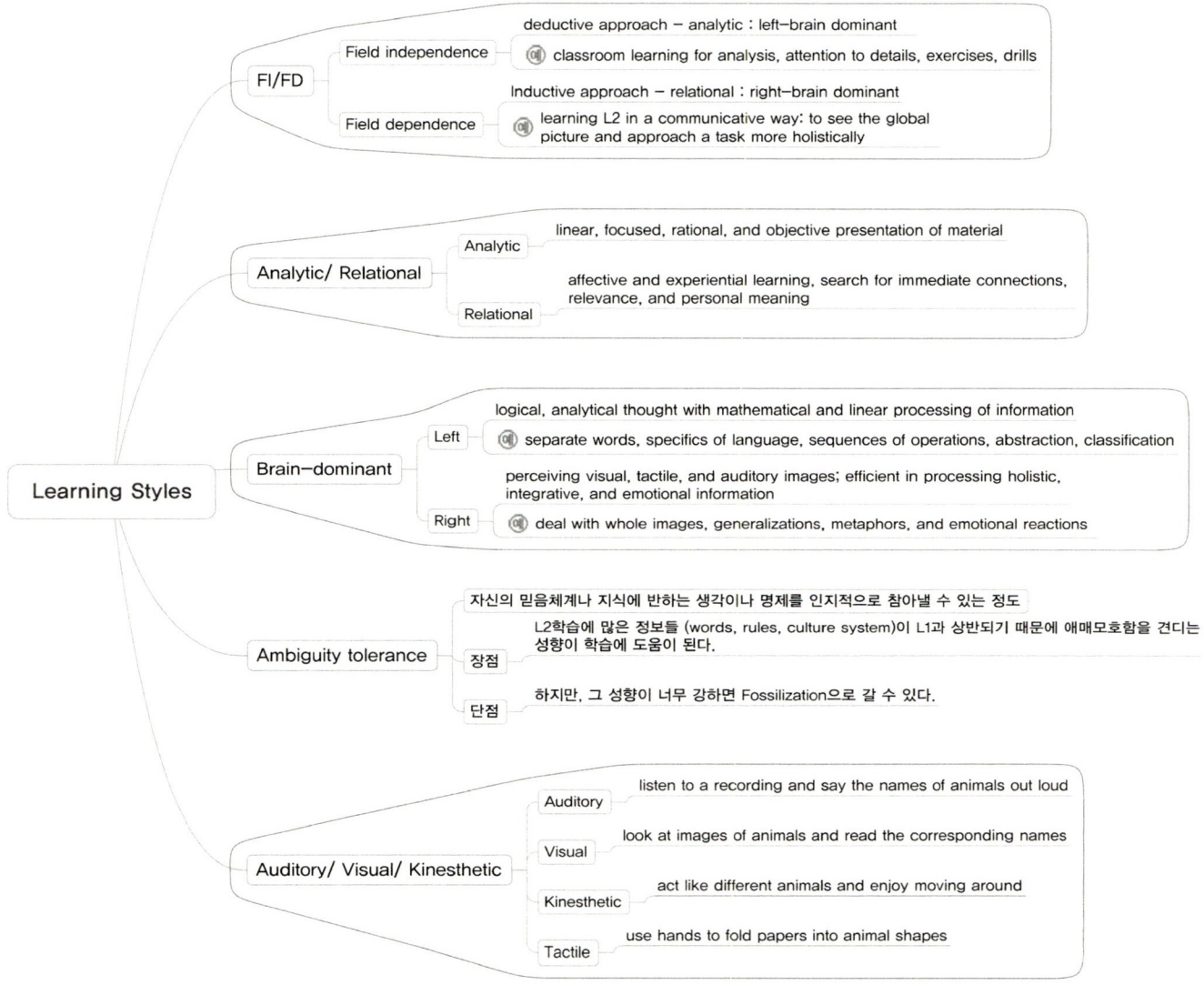

# 03 학습 전략

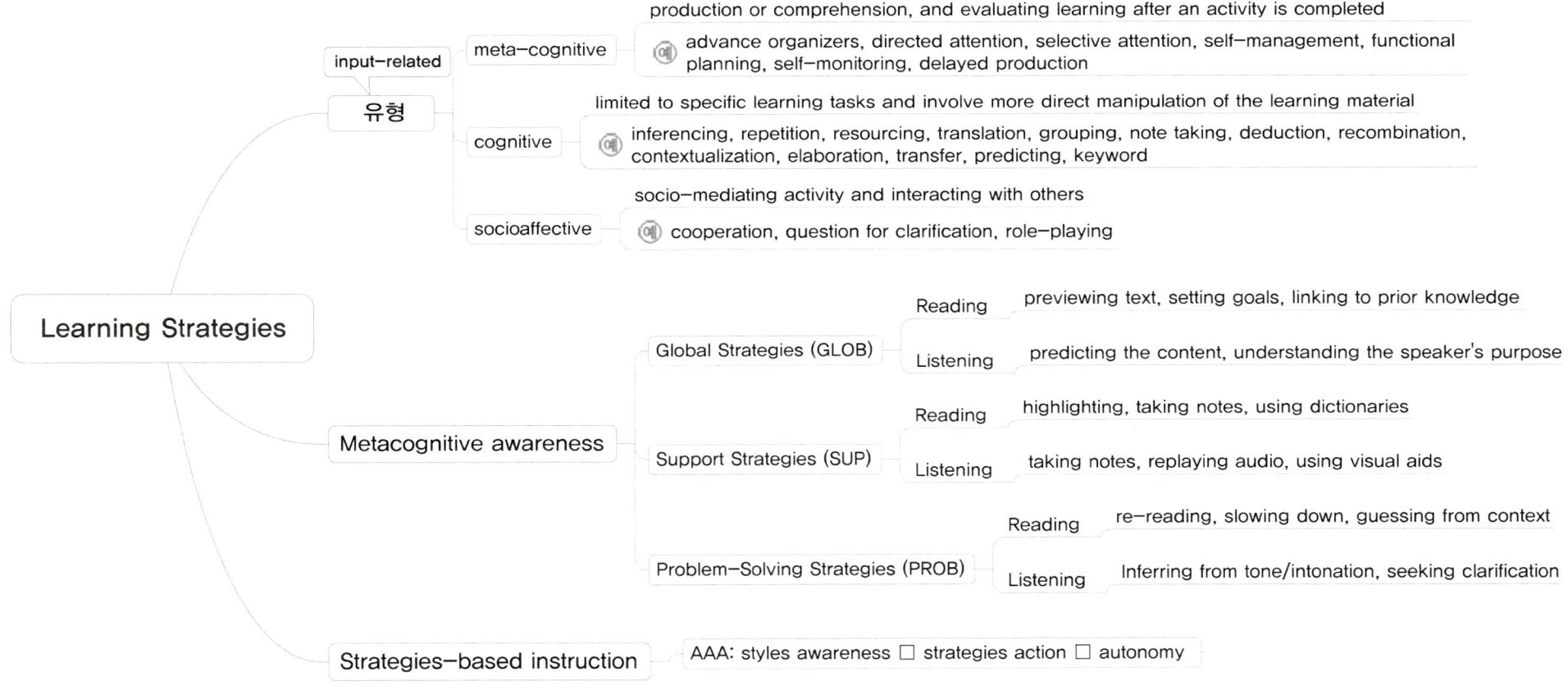

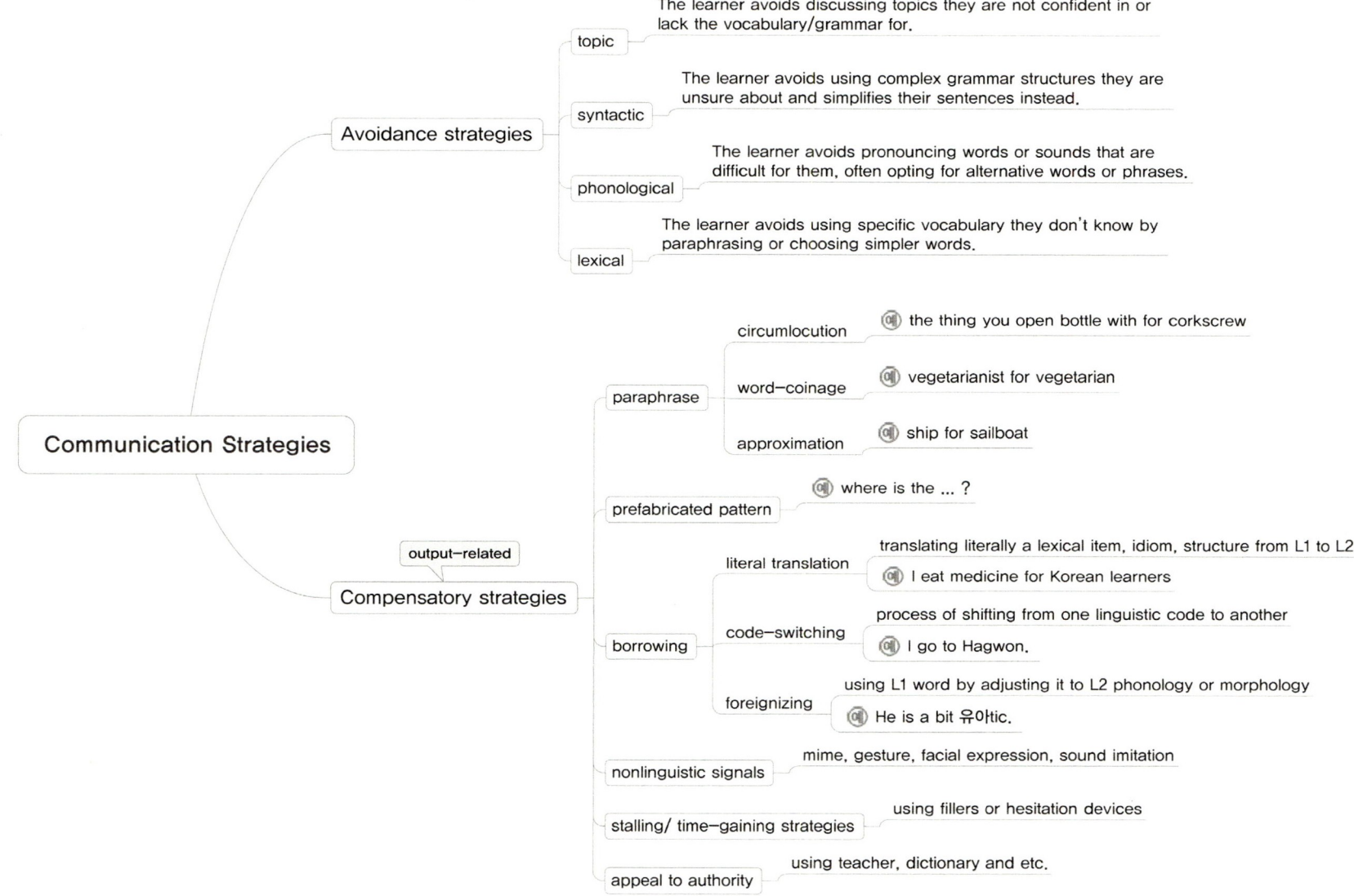

## 05 정의적 측면

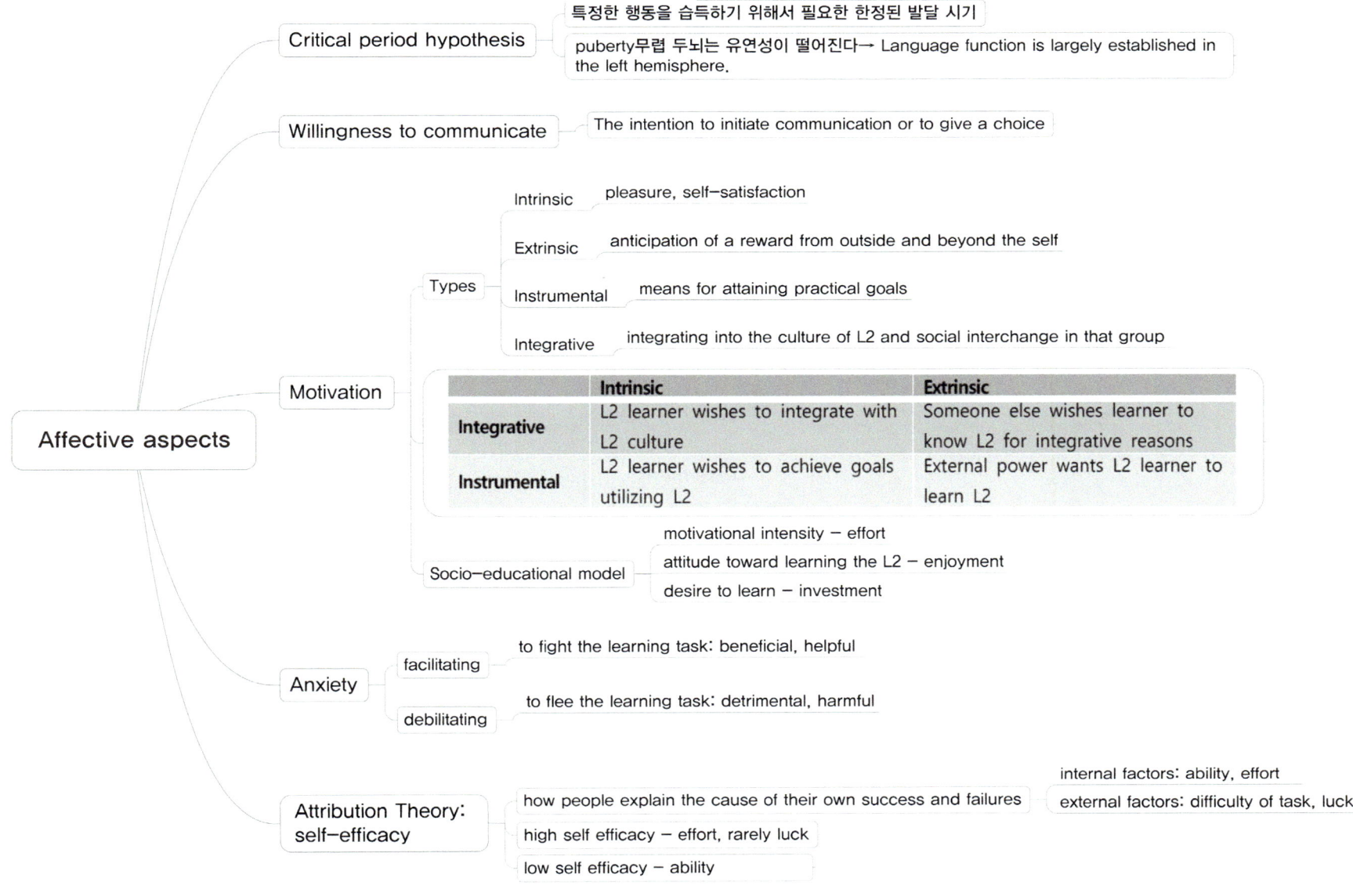

# 06 언어학습의 Agency

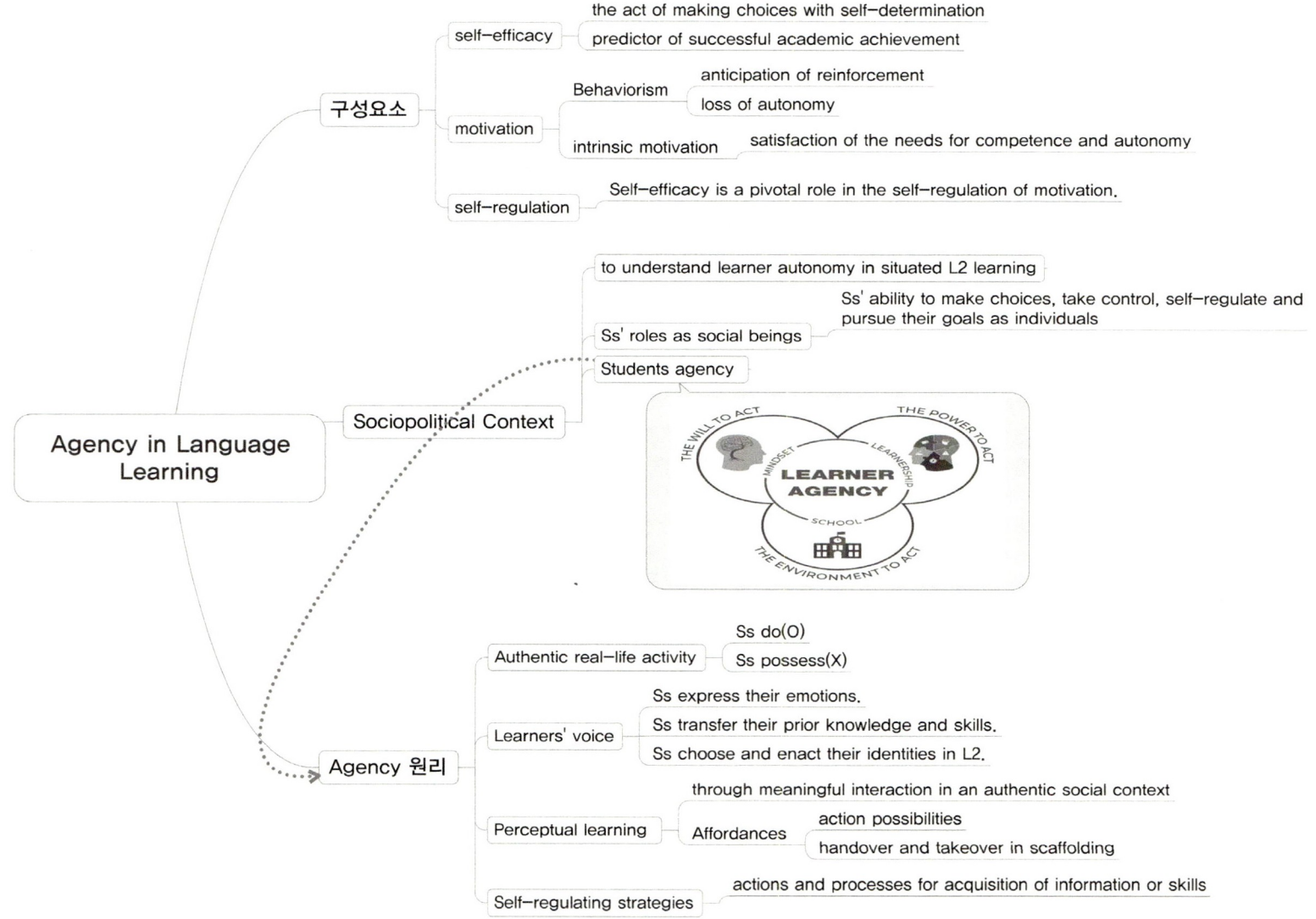

**Agency in Language Learning**

- 구성요소
  - self-efficacy
    - the act of making choices with self-determination
    - predictor of successful academic achievement
  - motivation
    - Behaviorism
      - anticipation of reinforcement
      - loss of autonomy
    - intrinsic motivation — satisfaction of the needs for competence and autonomy
  - self-regulation — Self-efficacy is a pivotal role in the self-regulation of motivation.

- Sociopolitical Context
  - to understand learner autonomy in situated L2 learning
  - Ss' roles as social beings — Ss' ability to make choices, take control, self-regulate and pursue their goals as individuals
  - Students agency

- Agency 원리
  - Authentic real-life activity
    - Ss do(O)
    - Ss possess(X)
  - Learners' voice
    - Ss express their emotions.
    - Ss transfer their prior knowledge and skills.
    - Ss choose and enact their identities in L2.
  - Perceptual learning
    - through meaningful interaction in an authentic social context
    - Affordances
      - action possibilities
      - handover and takeover in scaffolding
  - Self-regulating strategies — actions and processes for acquisition of information or skills

# 03.
# Communicative Competence

권영주 영어교육론 MIND MAP

# MEMO

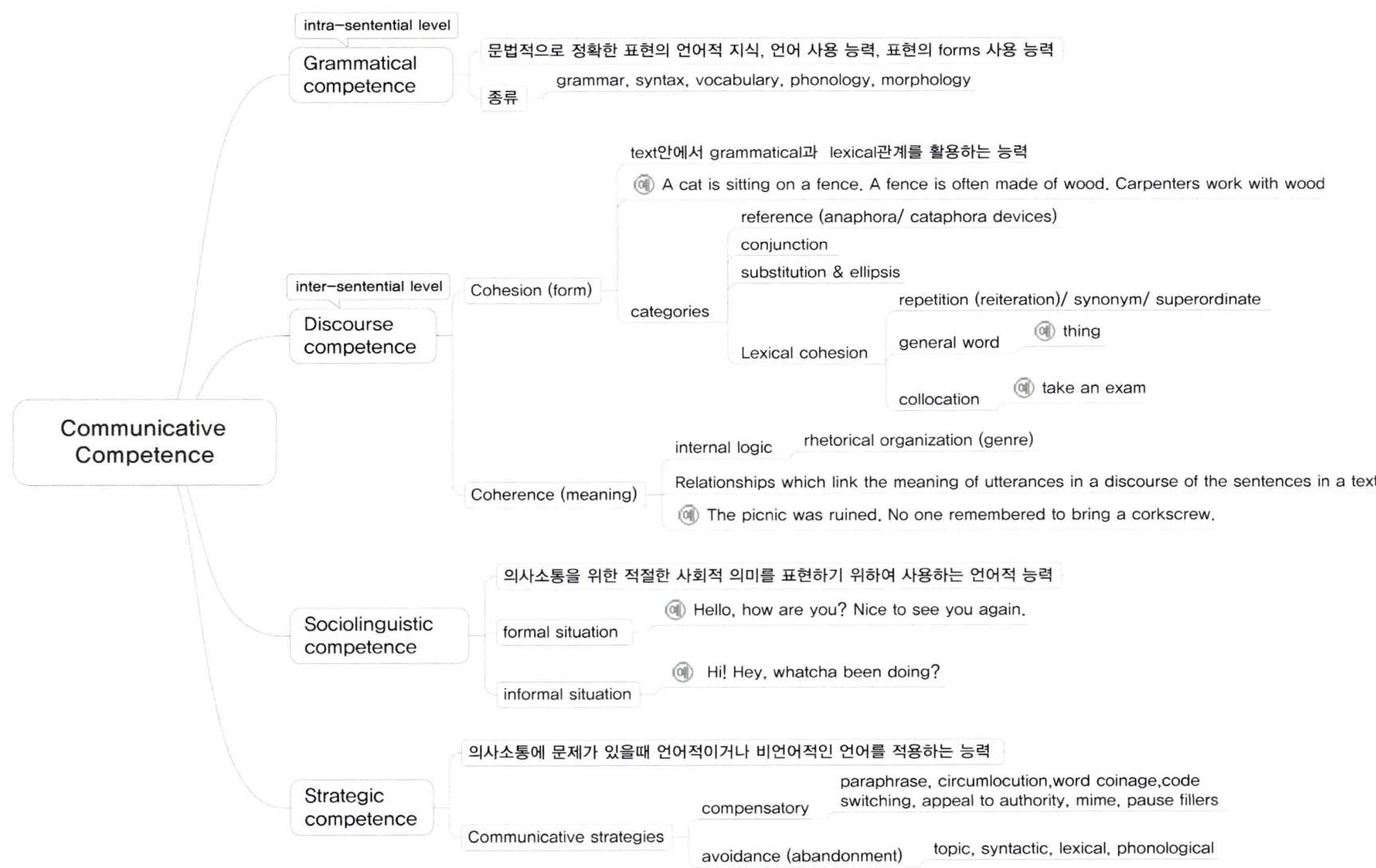

# 02 사회문화적 교수법

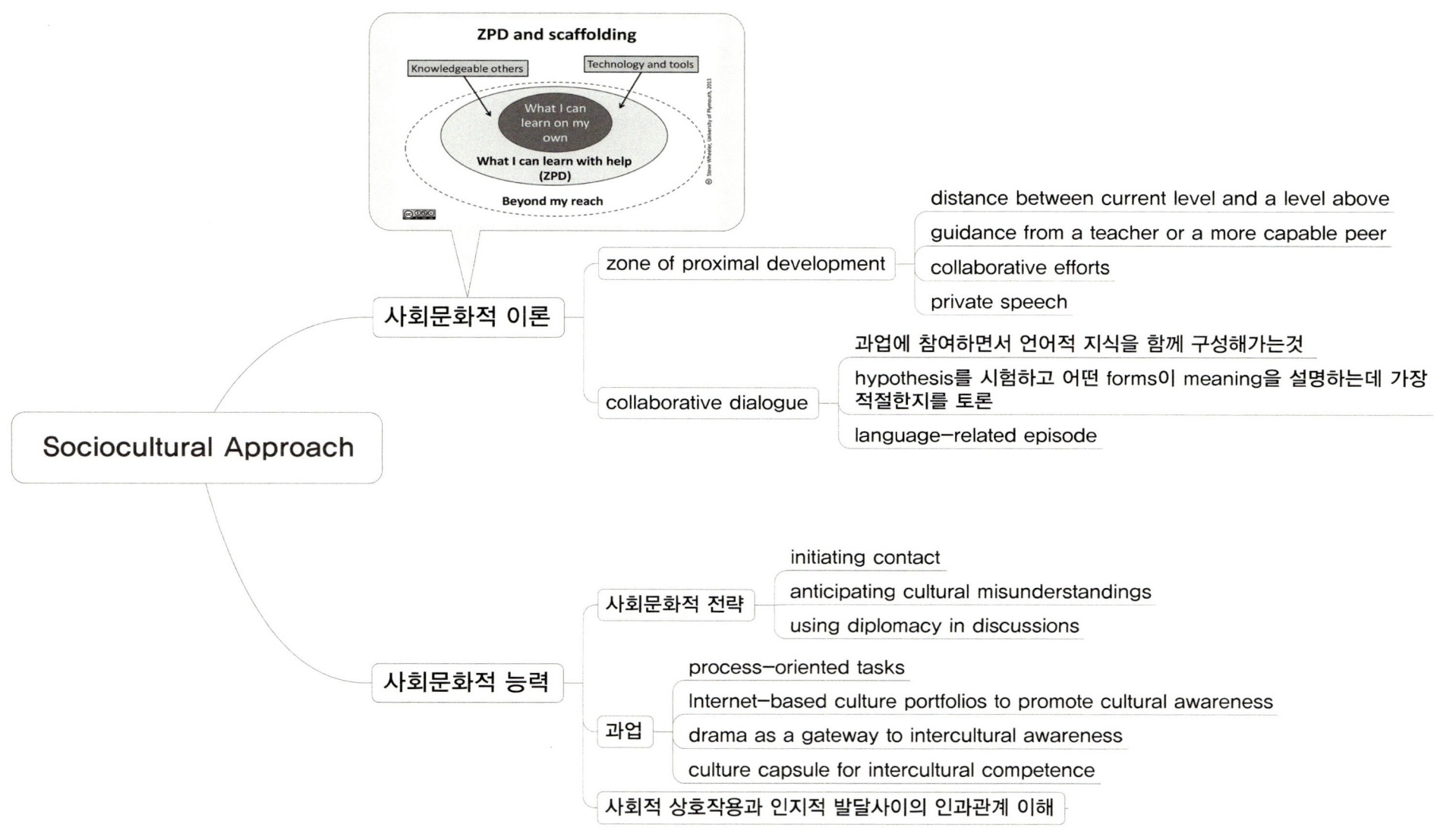

**Sociocultural Approach**

- 사회문화적 이론
  - zone of proximal development
    - distance between current level and a level above
    - guidance from a teacher or a more capable peer
    - collaborative efforts
    - private speech
  - collaborative dialogue
    - 과업에 참여하면서 언어적 지식을 함께 구성해가는것
    - hypothesis를 시험하고 어떤 forms이 meaning을 설명하는데 가장 적절한지를 토론
    - language-related episode

- 사회문화적 능력
  - 사회문화적 전략
    - initiating contact
    - anticipating cultural misunderstandings
    - using diplomacy in discussions
  - 과업
    - process-oriented tasks
    - Internet-based culture portfolios to promote cultural awareness
    - drama as a gateway to intercultural awareness
    - culture capsule for intercultural competence
  - 사회적 상호작용과 인지적 발달사이의 인과관계 이해

# 03 화용론

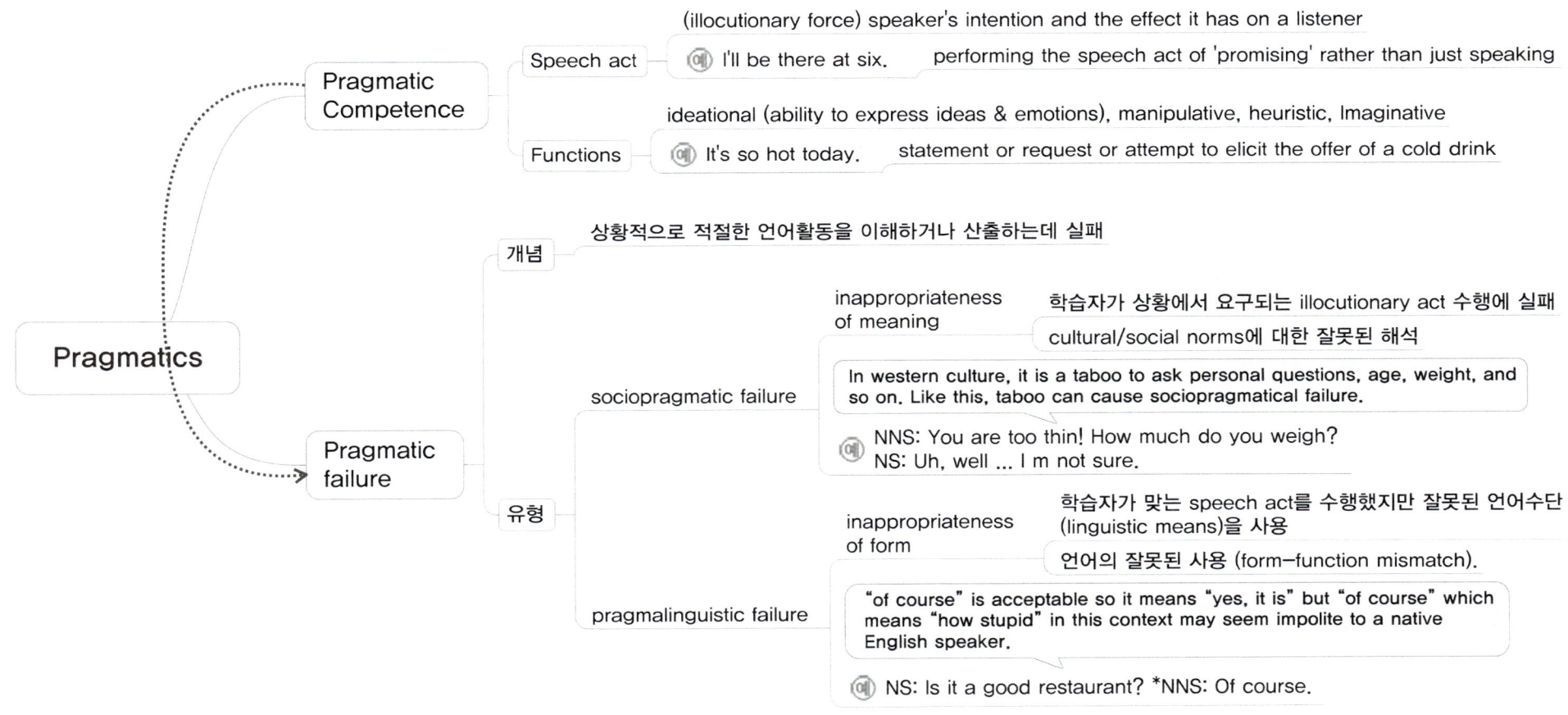

# 04 의미 협상

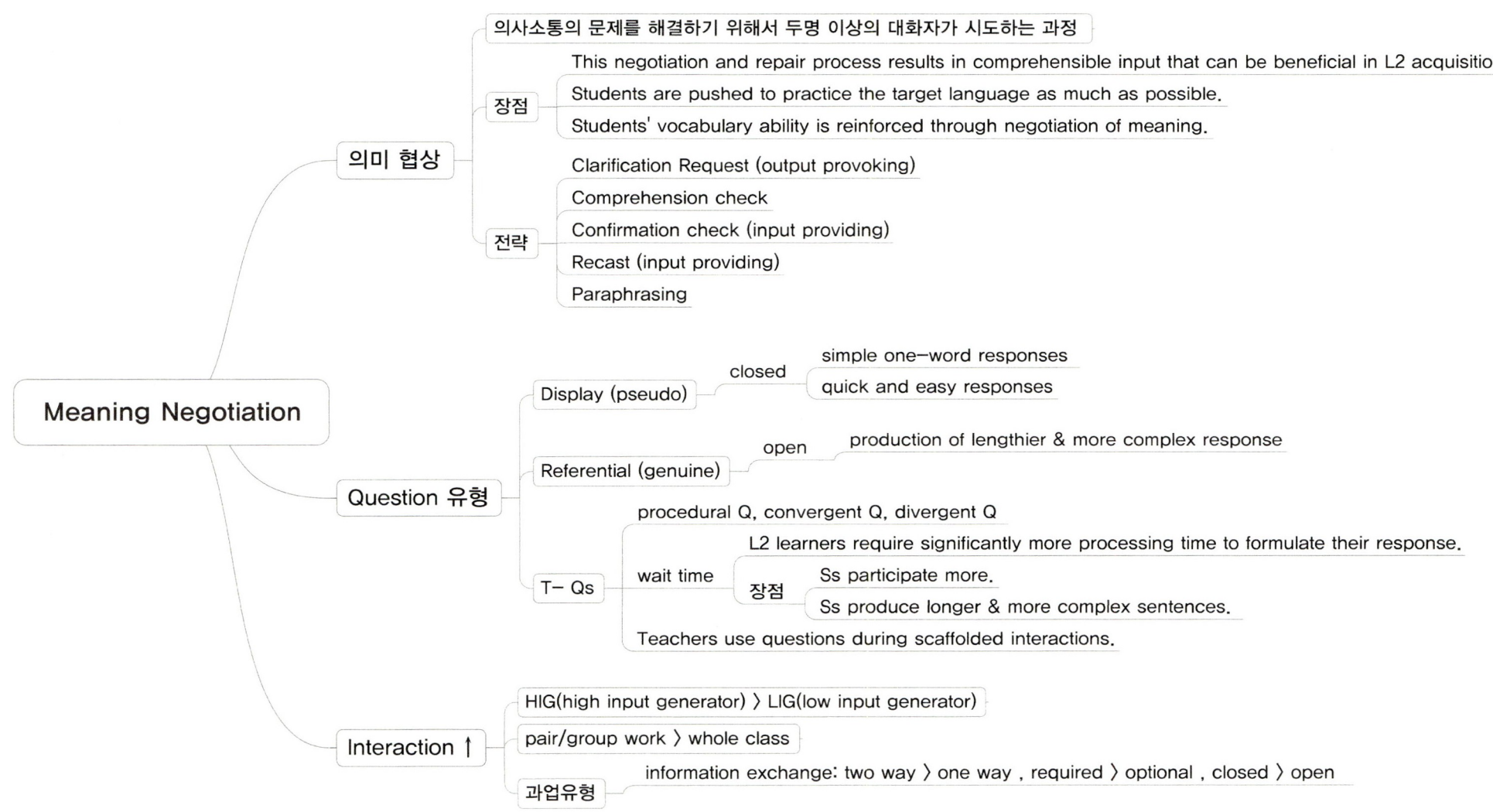

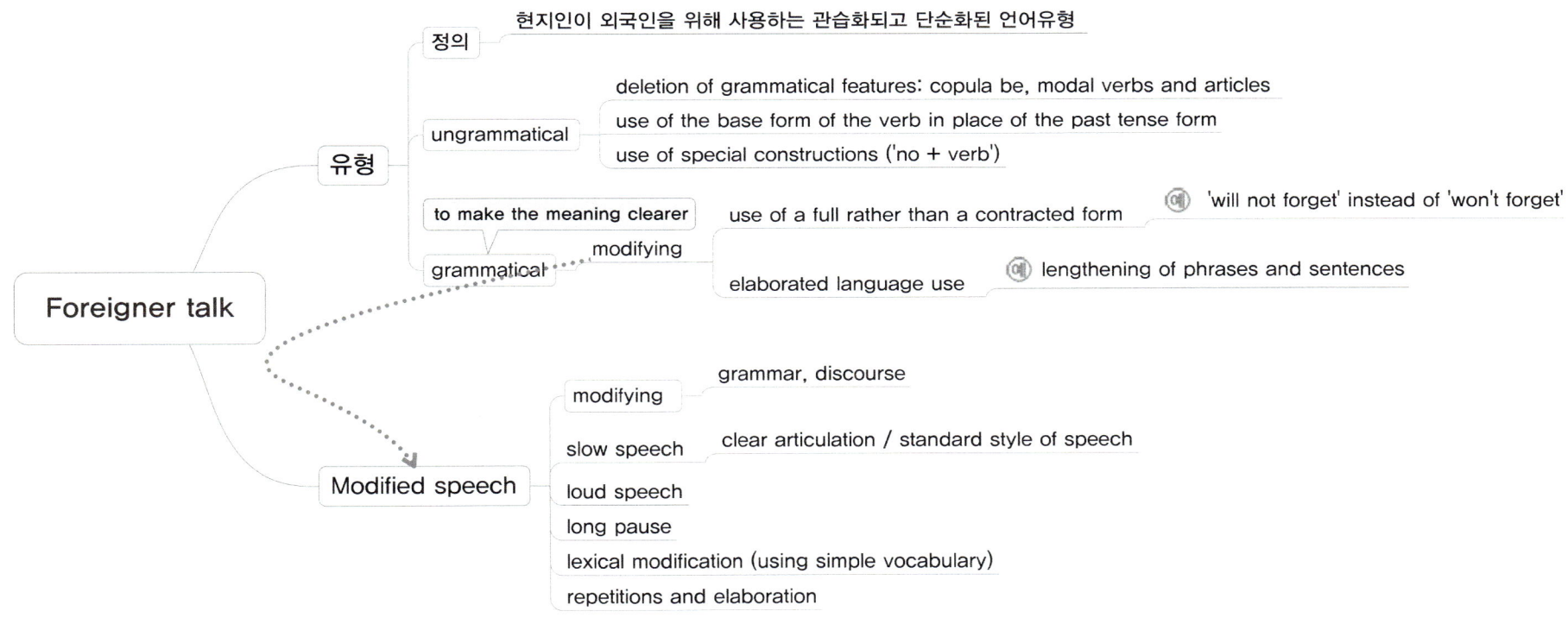

# 06 학습자 언어

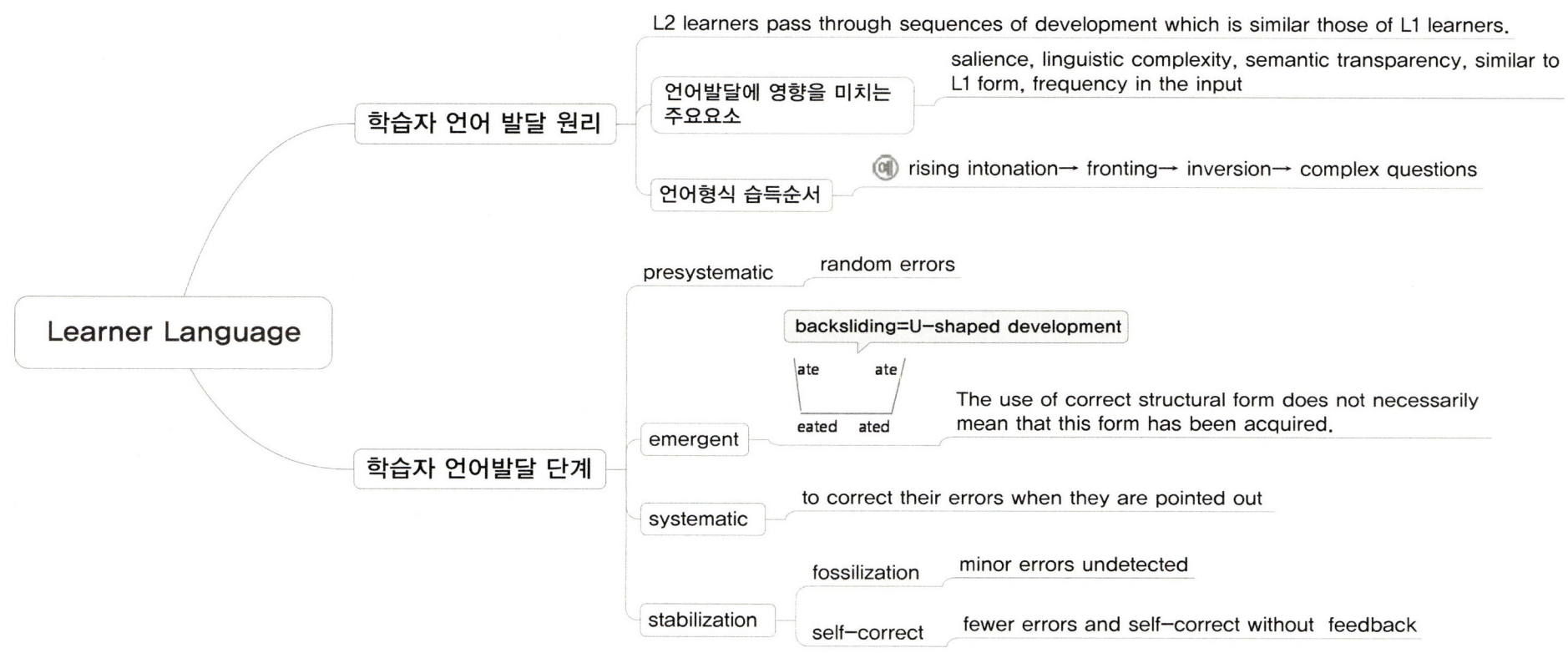

# 07 오류 분석

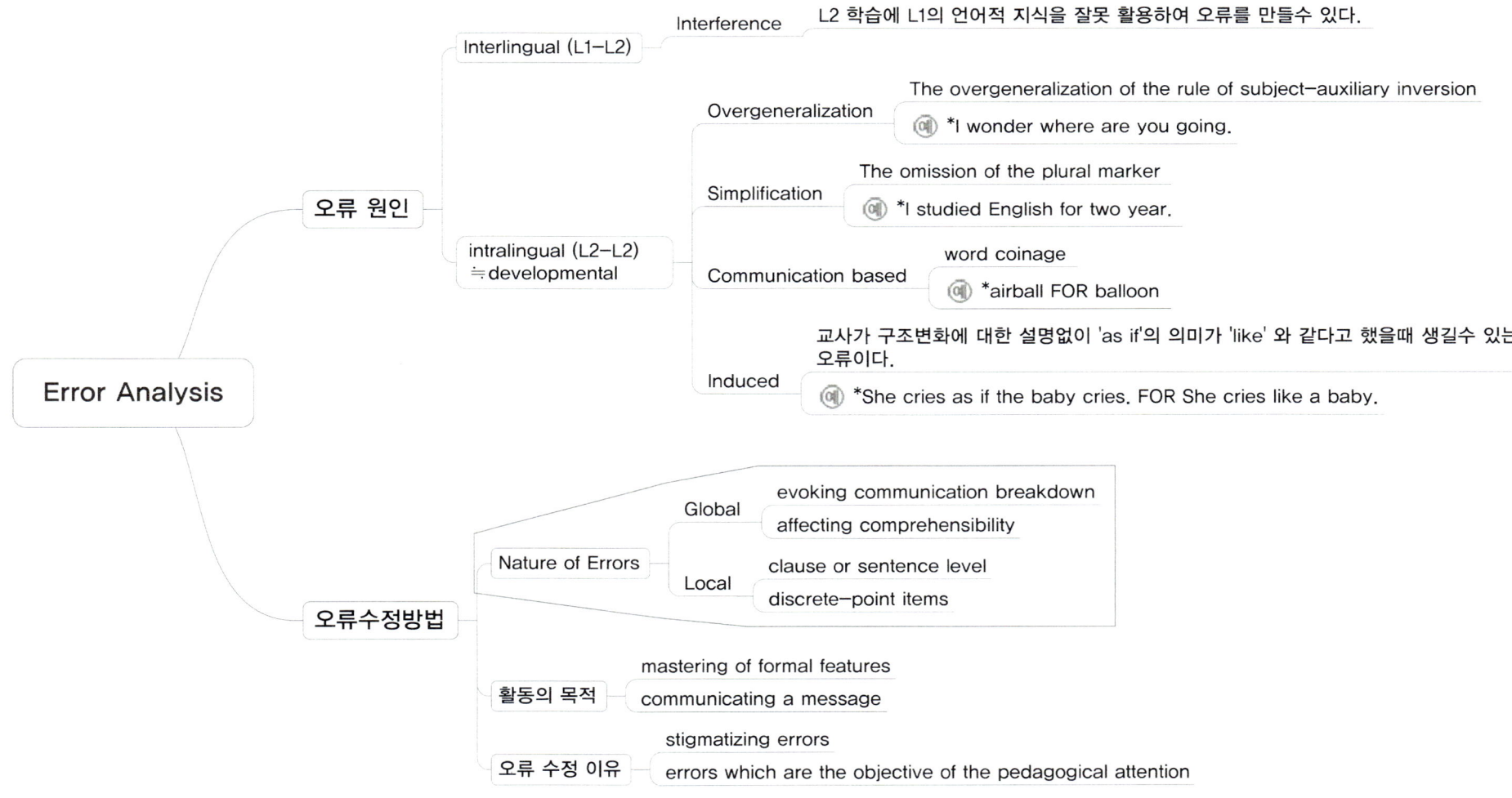

# 08 피드백

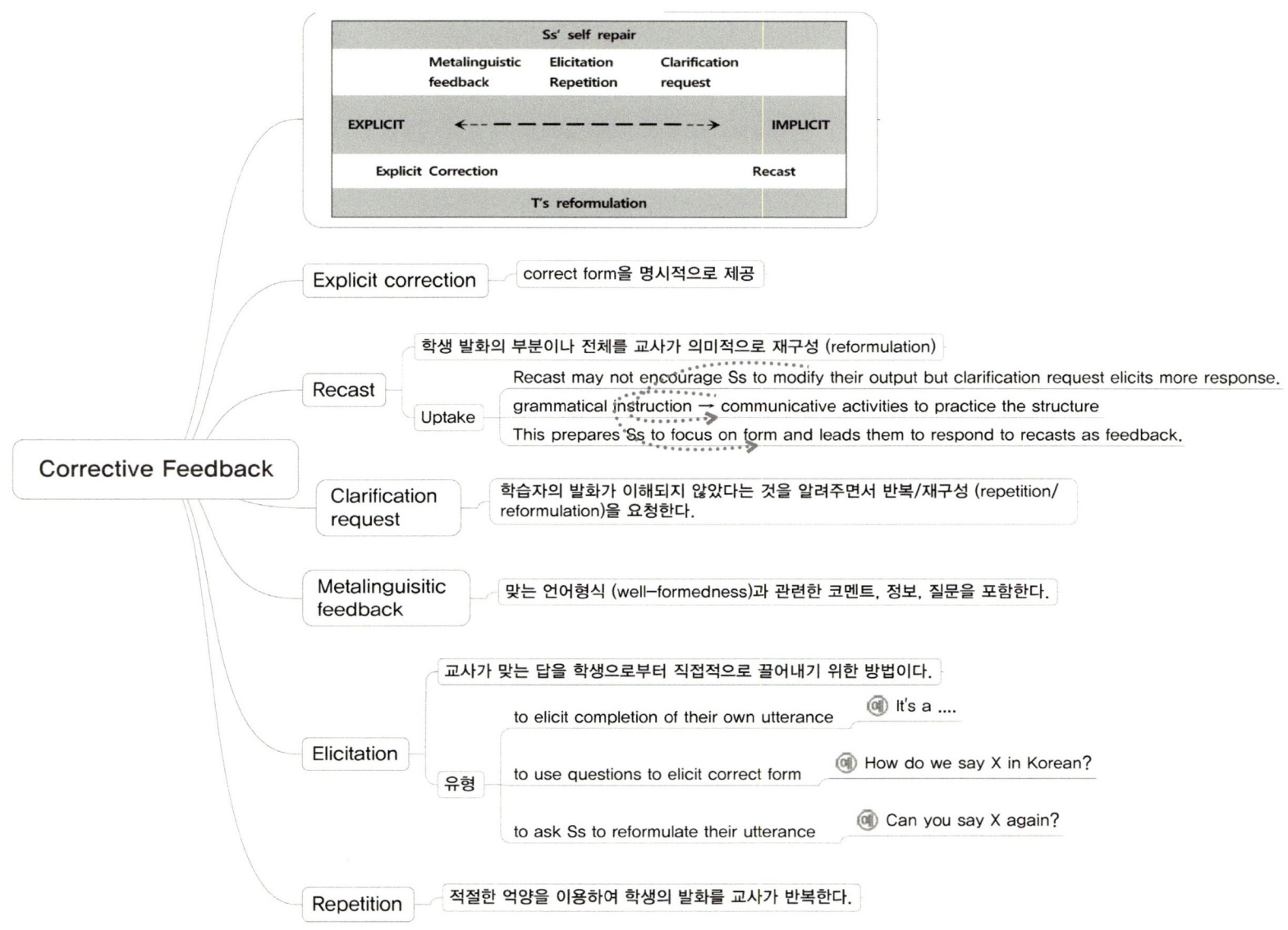

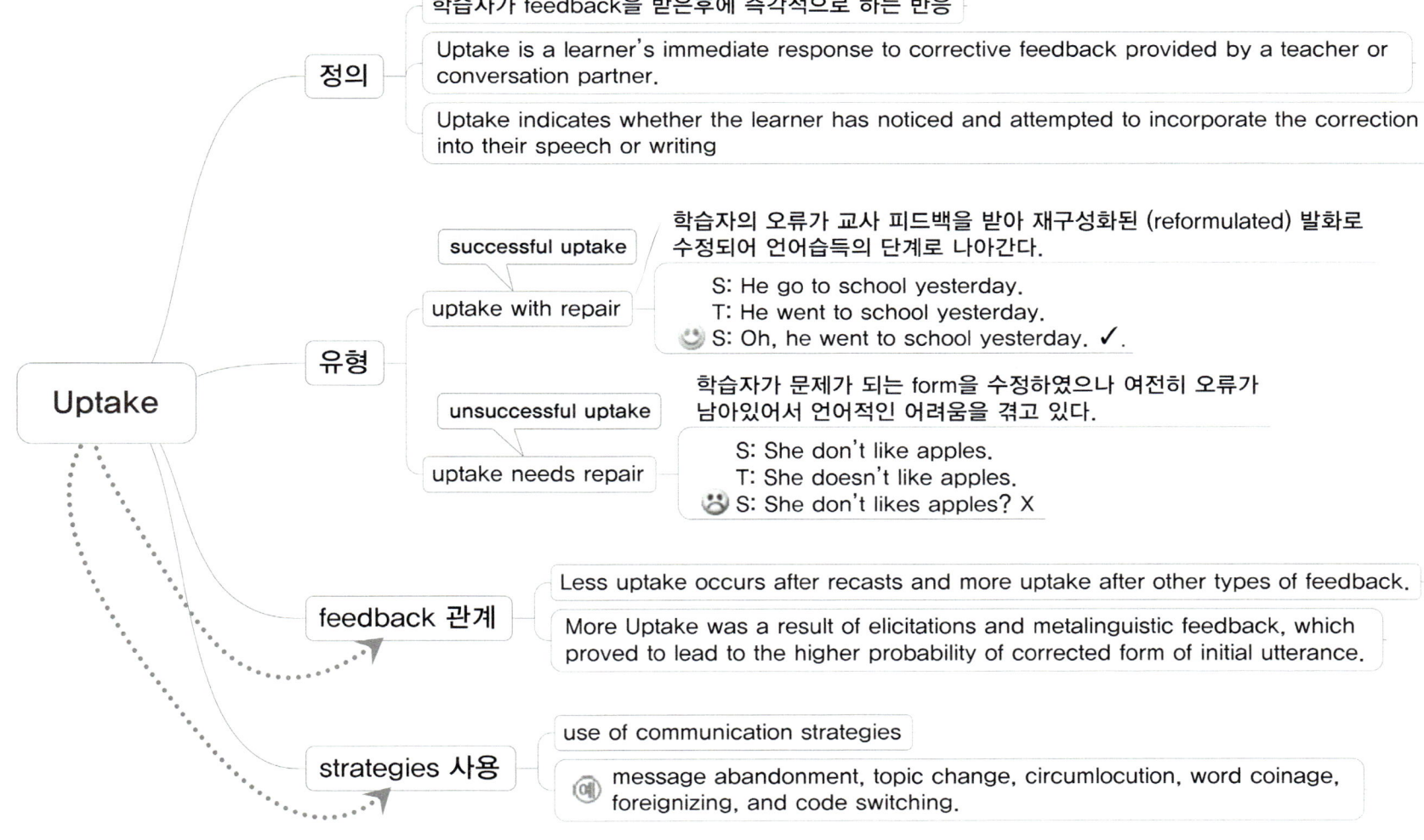

# 10 증거

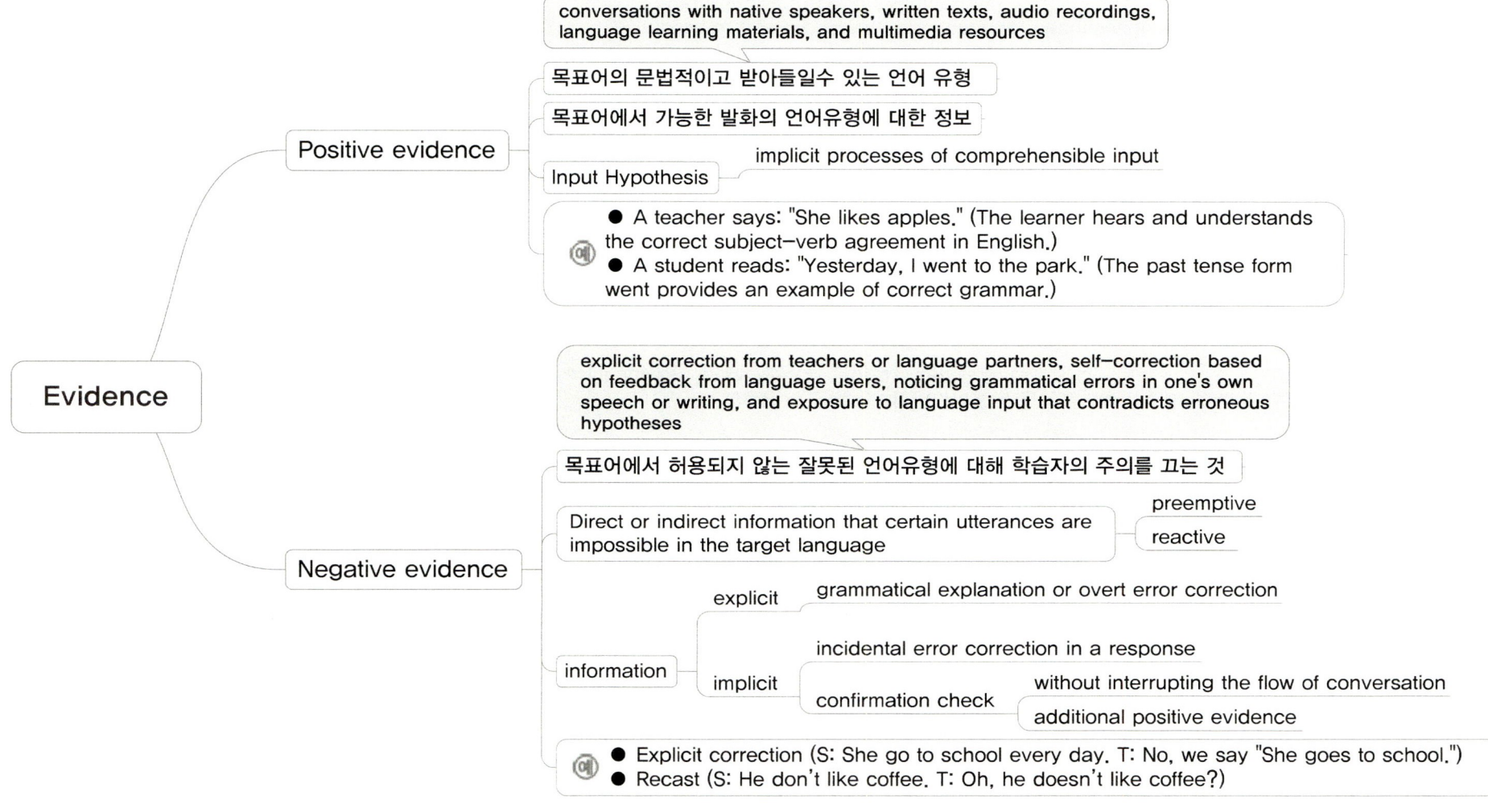

# 04.
# Language Teaching Methodology

권영주 영어교육론 MIND MAP

# MEMO

# 01 언어학습 교수법

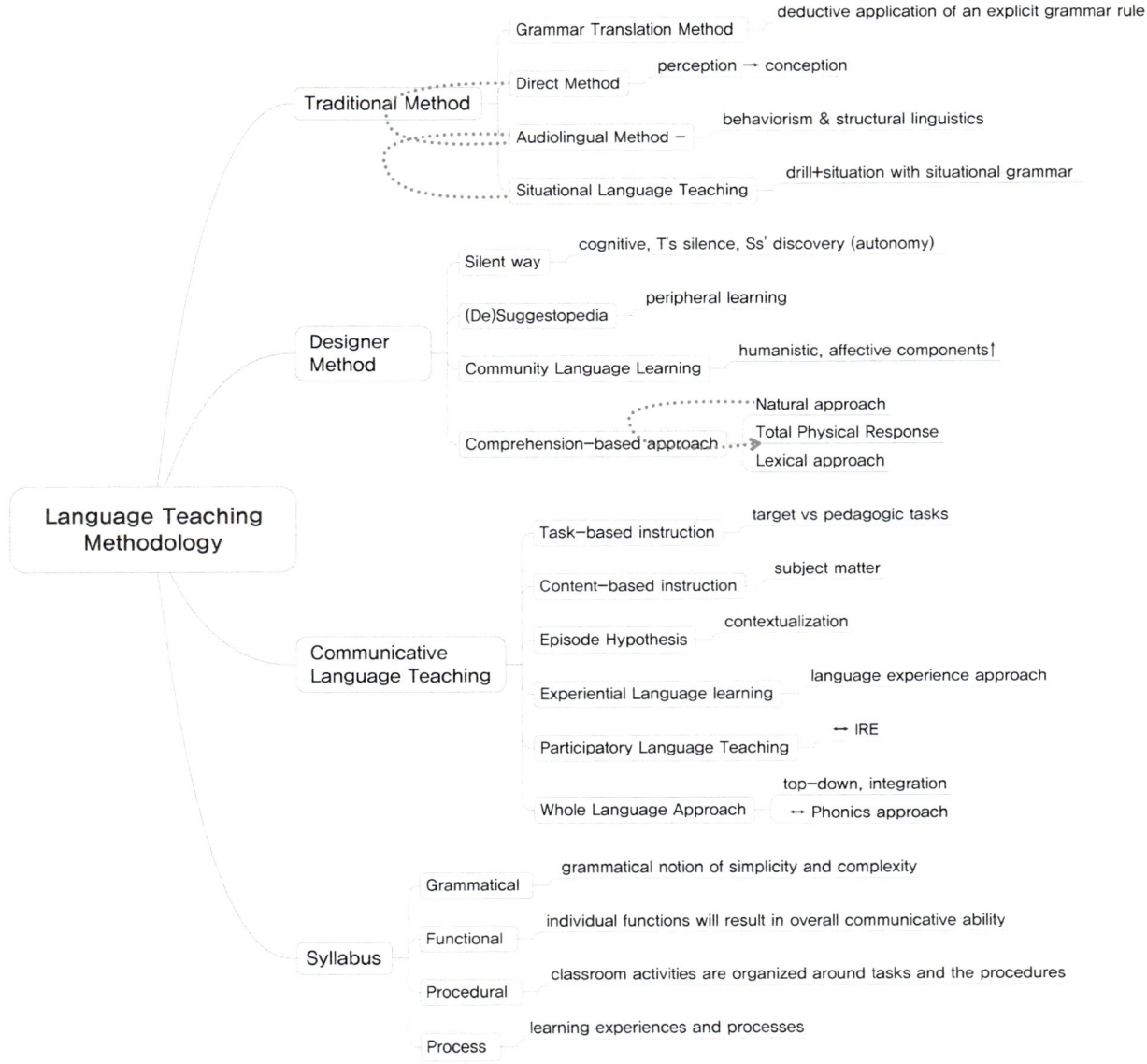

## 02 교수 요목

| option 1 | option 2 | option 3 |
|---|---|---|
| synthetic | analytic | analytic |
| focus on forms | focus on meaning | focus on form |
| GTM, ALM, TPR, Silent way | Natural approach Immersion | TBLT, CBLT |
| structural/ N-F syllabus | procedural syllabus | process syllabus |

**Teaching Syllabus**

- **Grammatical**
  - 입력이 문법의 단순함과 복잡함에 따라 선택되고 등급이 매겨진다.
  - 언어는 meaning을 만들기 위해서 여러가지 방법으로 만들어질 수 있는 한정된 rules로 구성된다.

- **Functional**
  - to use a language for social survival and travel purpose
  - 개별 기능이 더해지면 전체적인 의사소통 능력을 만든다는 가정에서 의사소통 능력(communicative competence)의 개념을 분석한다.

- **Process**
  - 수업활동은 과업 (tasks)과 그것들을 성취하기 위한 절차 (process)로 구성되어 있다.
  - 명시적인 문법수업이나 오류수정은 존재하지 않는다.
  - 의미 중심 교수요목: 의미협상과 의사소통 성취가 2언어습득을 하기 위해서 사용된다.
  - 학습 결과 (outcome) 보다는 학습자의 경험과 과정 (process)을 구체화한다.

## 03 전통적 교수법

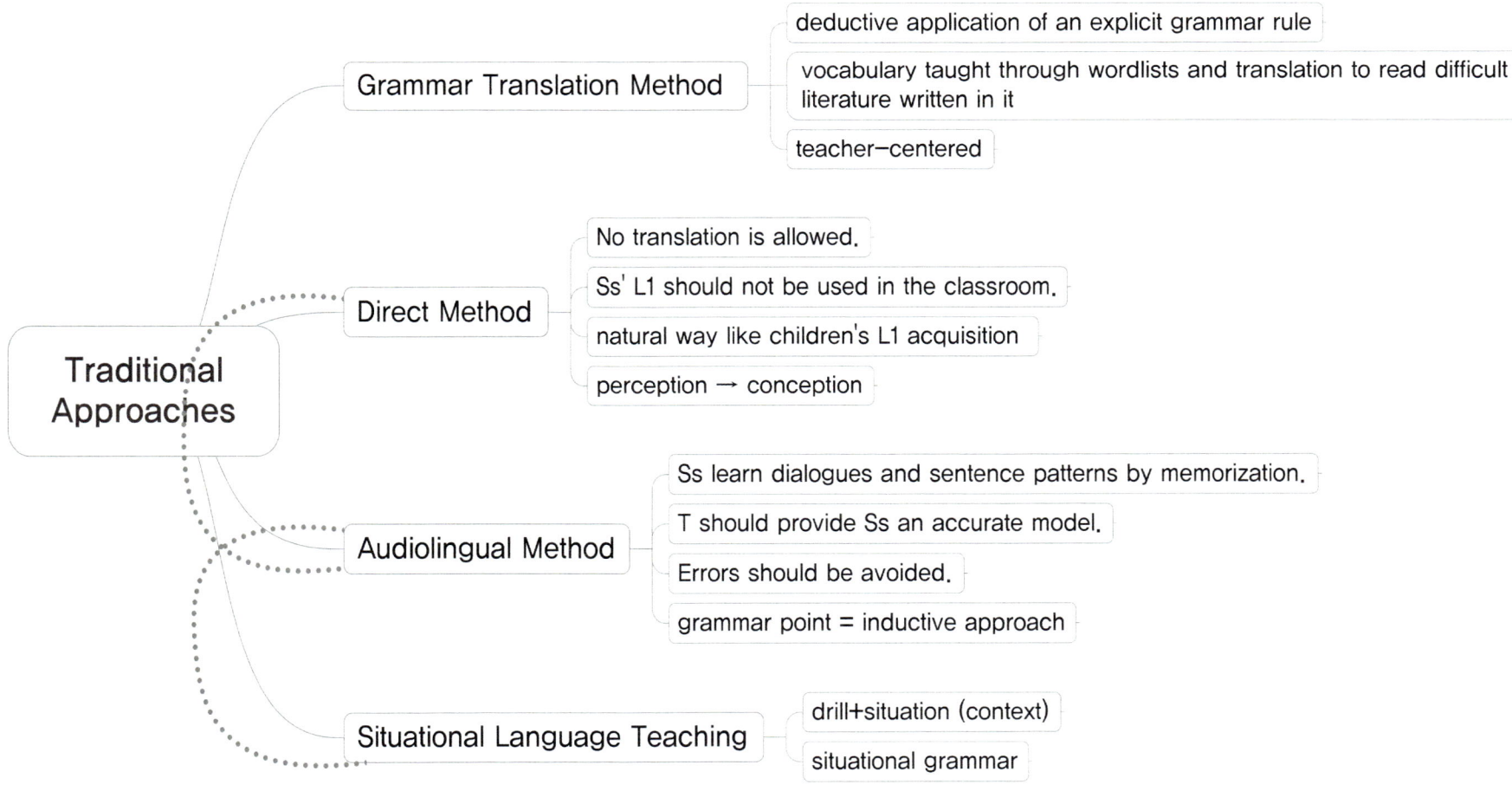

## 04 디자이너 교수법

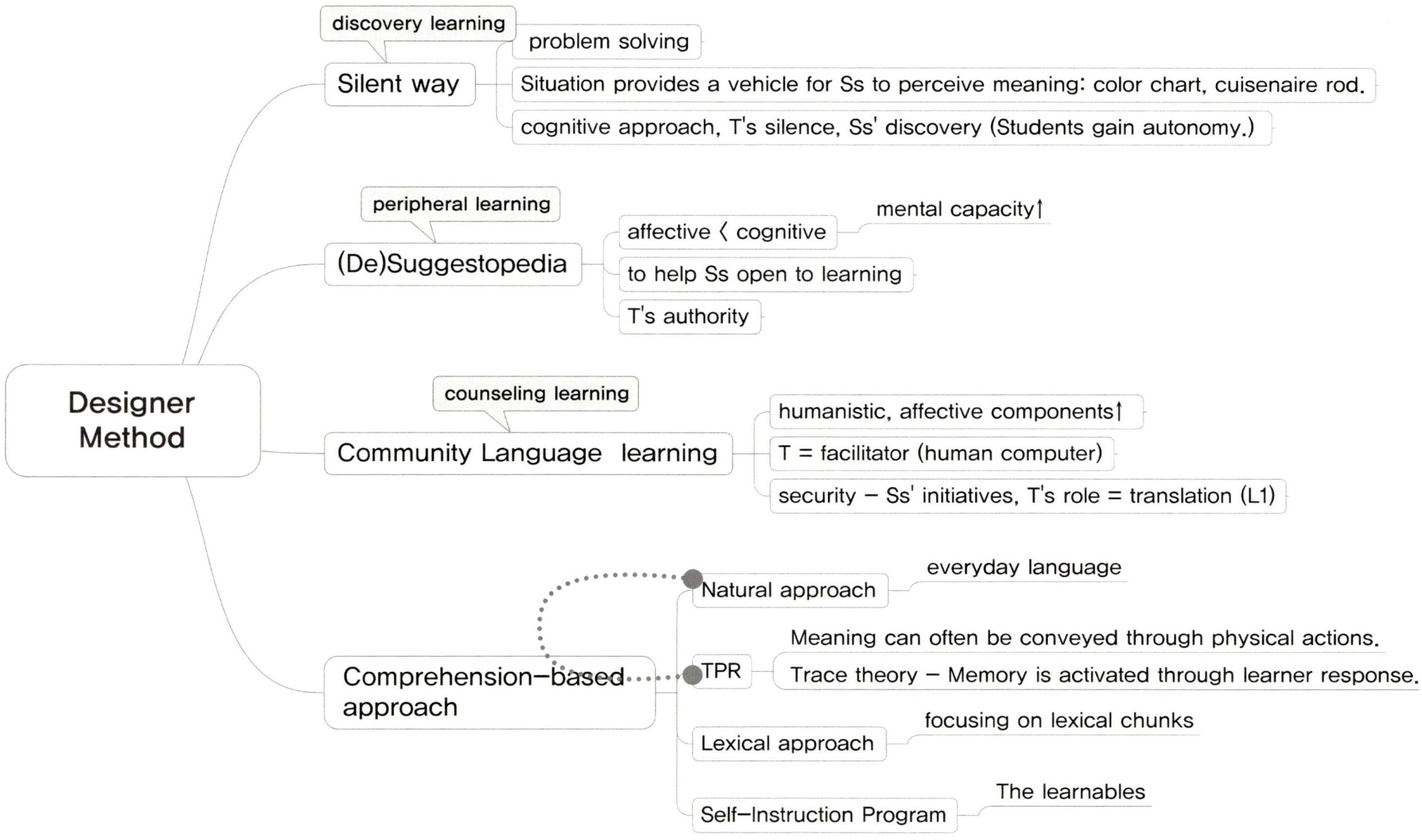

# 05 의사소통 교수법

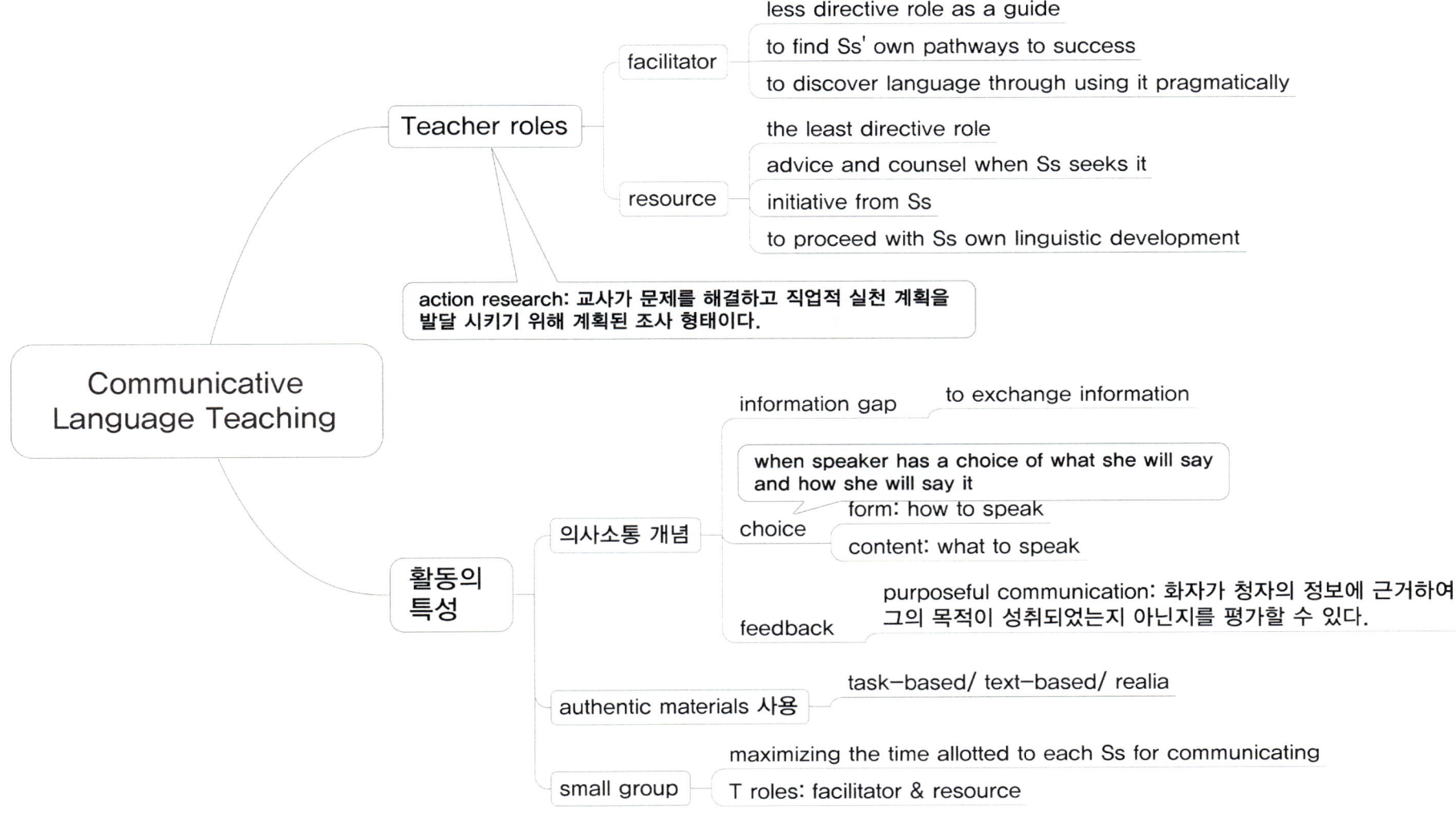

# 06 의사소통 활동

**Communicative Techniques**

- **Scrambled sentences** — teaching cohesion (form) & coherence (meaning)

- **Language games** — enjoyable and valuable communicative practice

- **Picture strip story**
  - example of problem-solving task
  - showing 1st picture and predicting 2nd
  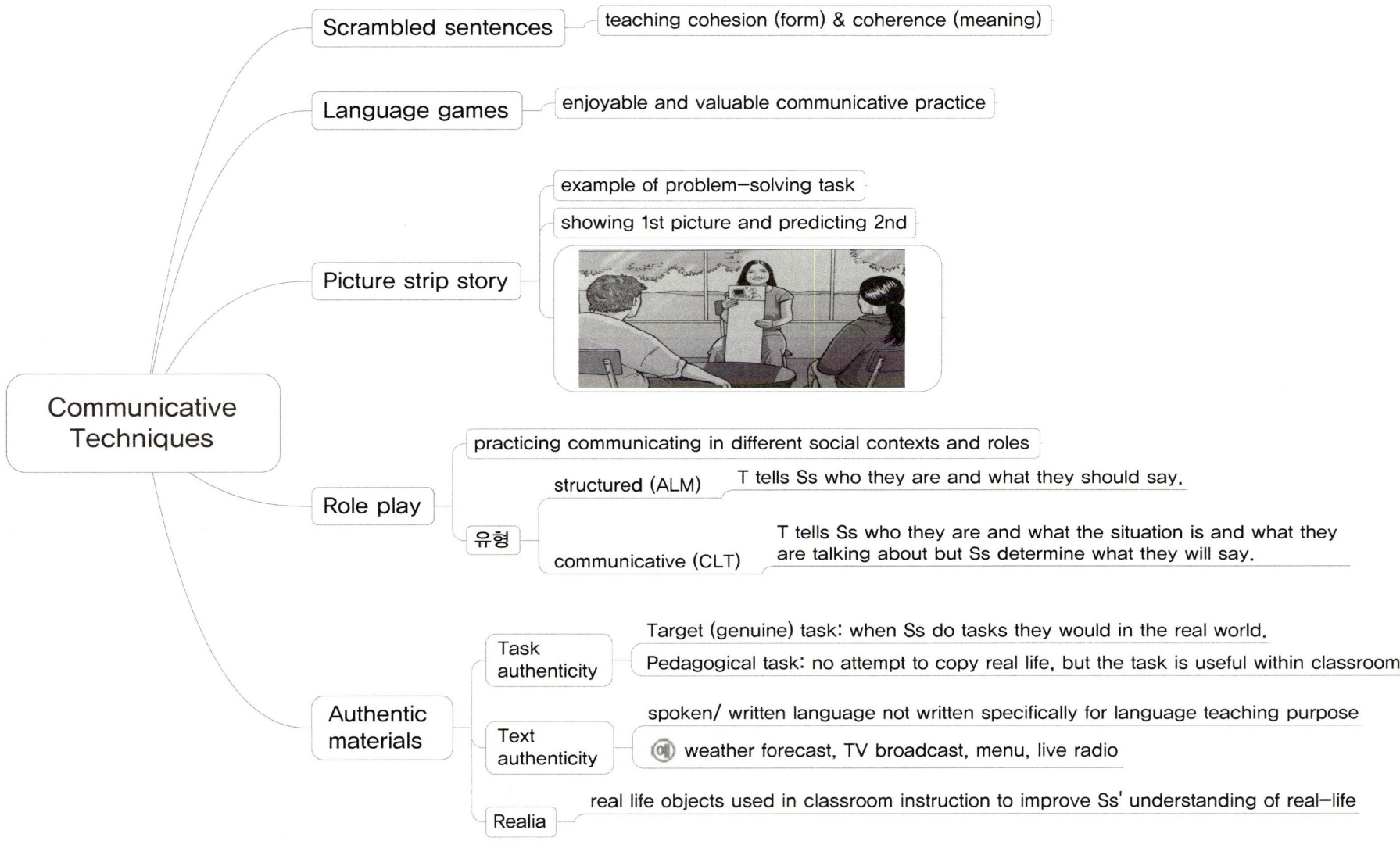

- **Role play**
  - practicing communicating in different social contexts and roles
  - 유형
    - structured (ALM): T tells Ss who they are and what they should say.
    - communicative (CLT): T tells Ss who they are and what the situation is and what they are talking about but Ss determine what they will say.

- **Authentic materials**
  - Task authenticity
    - Target (genuine) task: when Ss do tasks they would in the real world.
    - Pedagogical task: no attempt to copy real life, but the task is useful within classroom
  - Text authenticity
    - spoken/ written language not written specifically for language teaching purpose
    - 예) weather forecast, TV broadcast, menu, live radio
  - Realia — real life objects used in classroom instruction to improve Ss' understanding of real-life

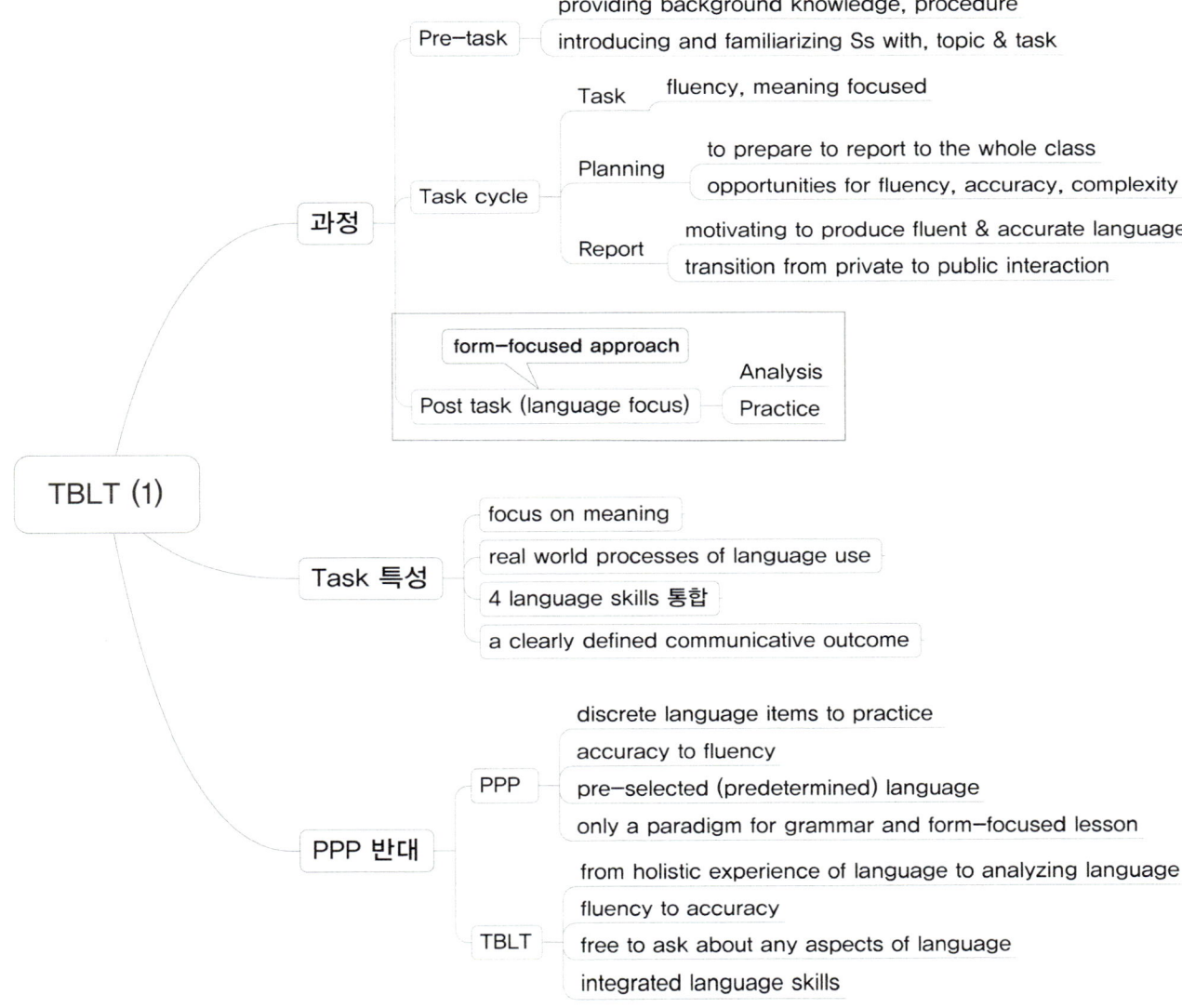

# 08 과업중심 교수법 (2)

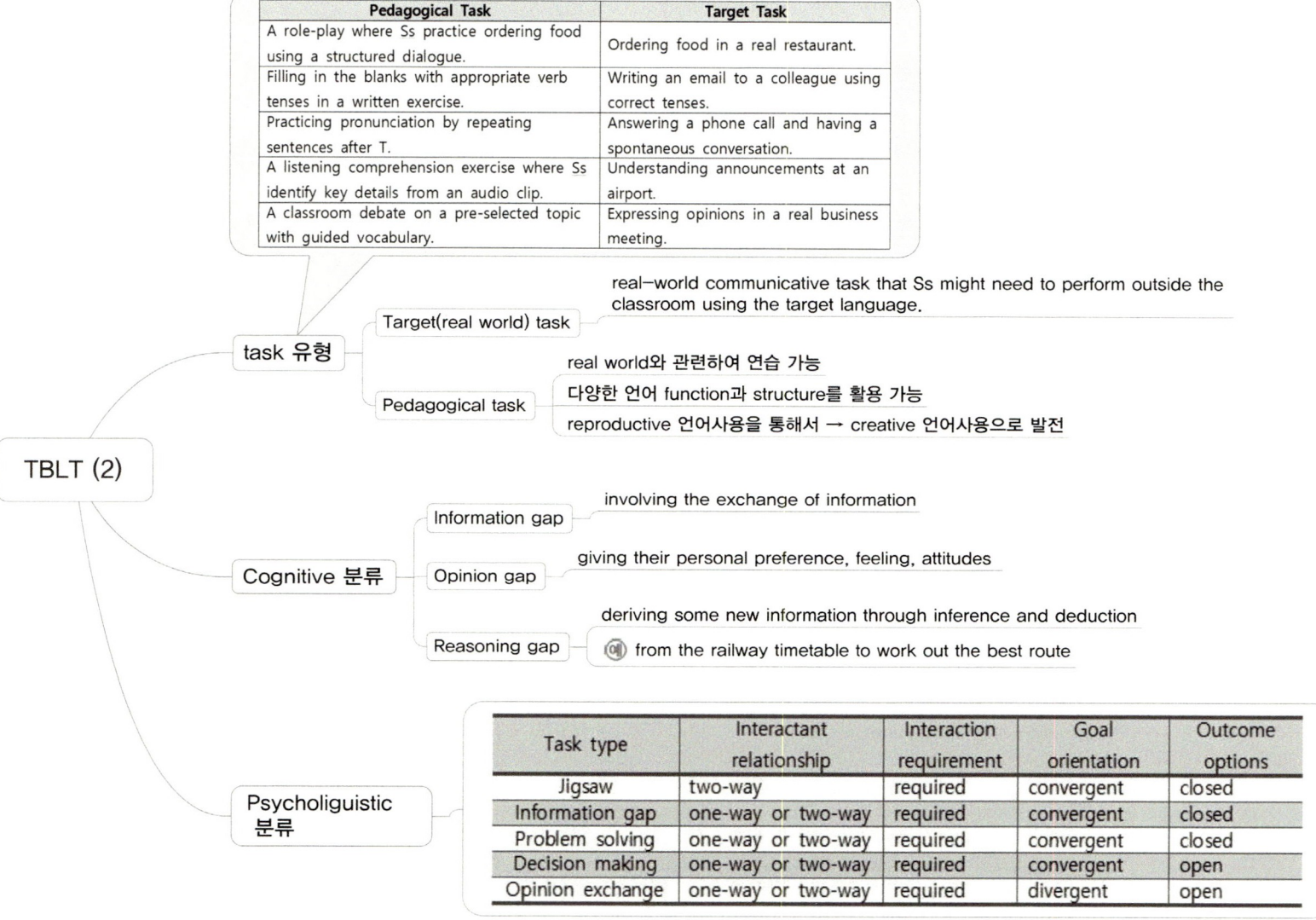

## 09 과업중심 교수법 (3)

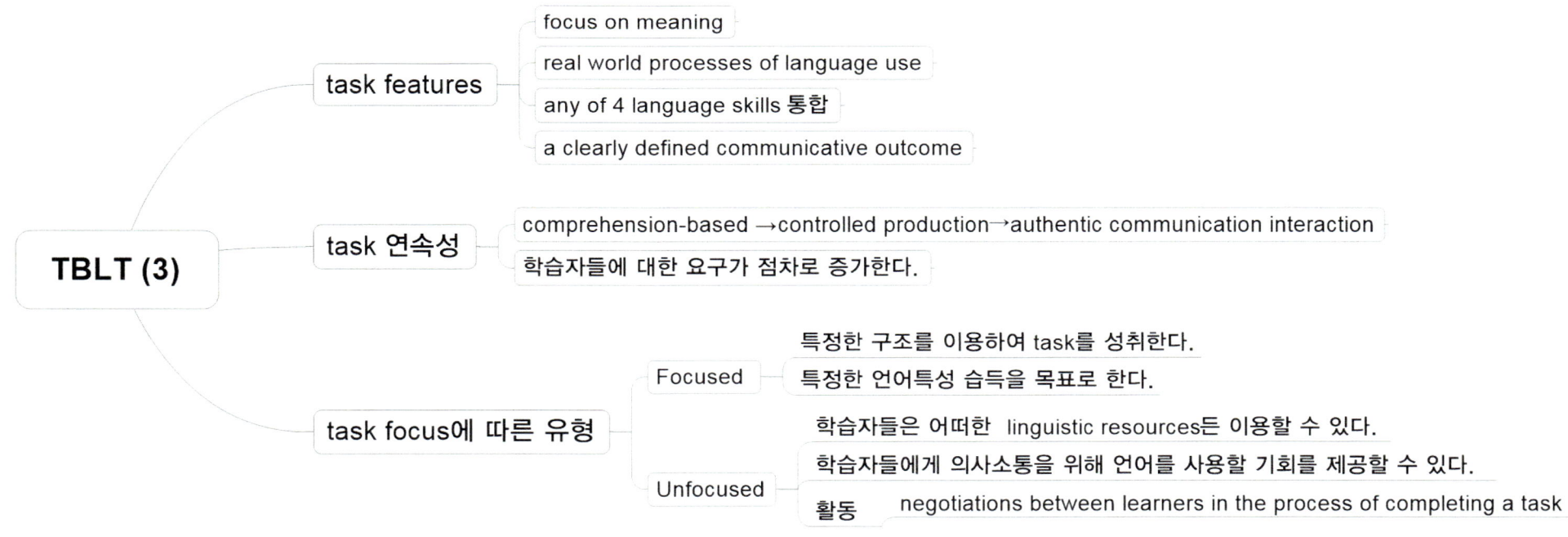

# 10 내용중심 교수법

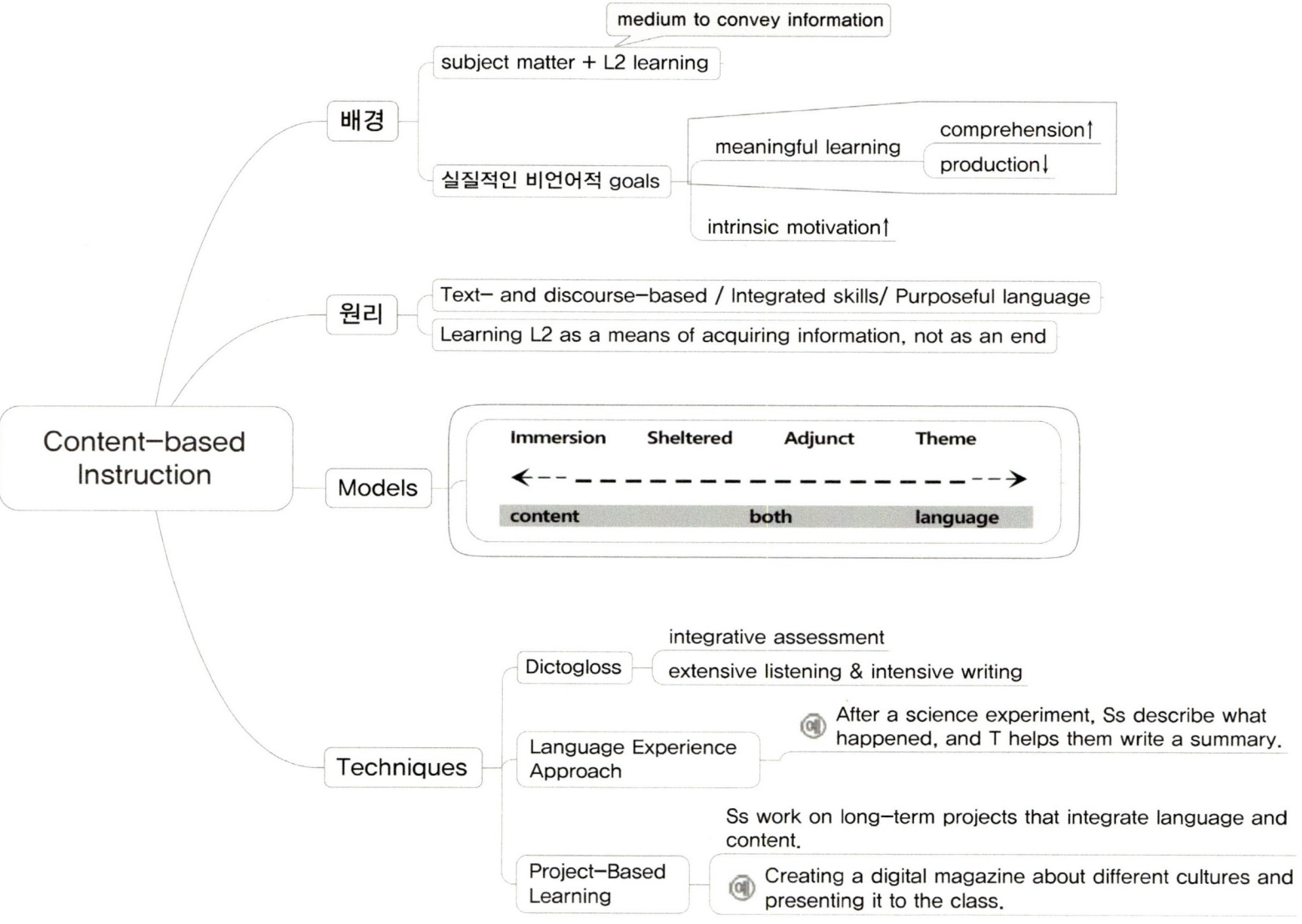

# 11 참여언어 교수법

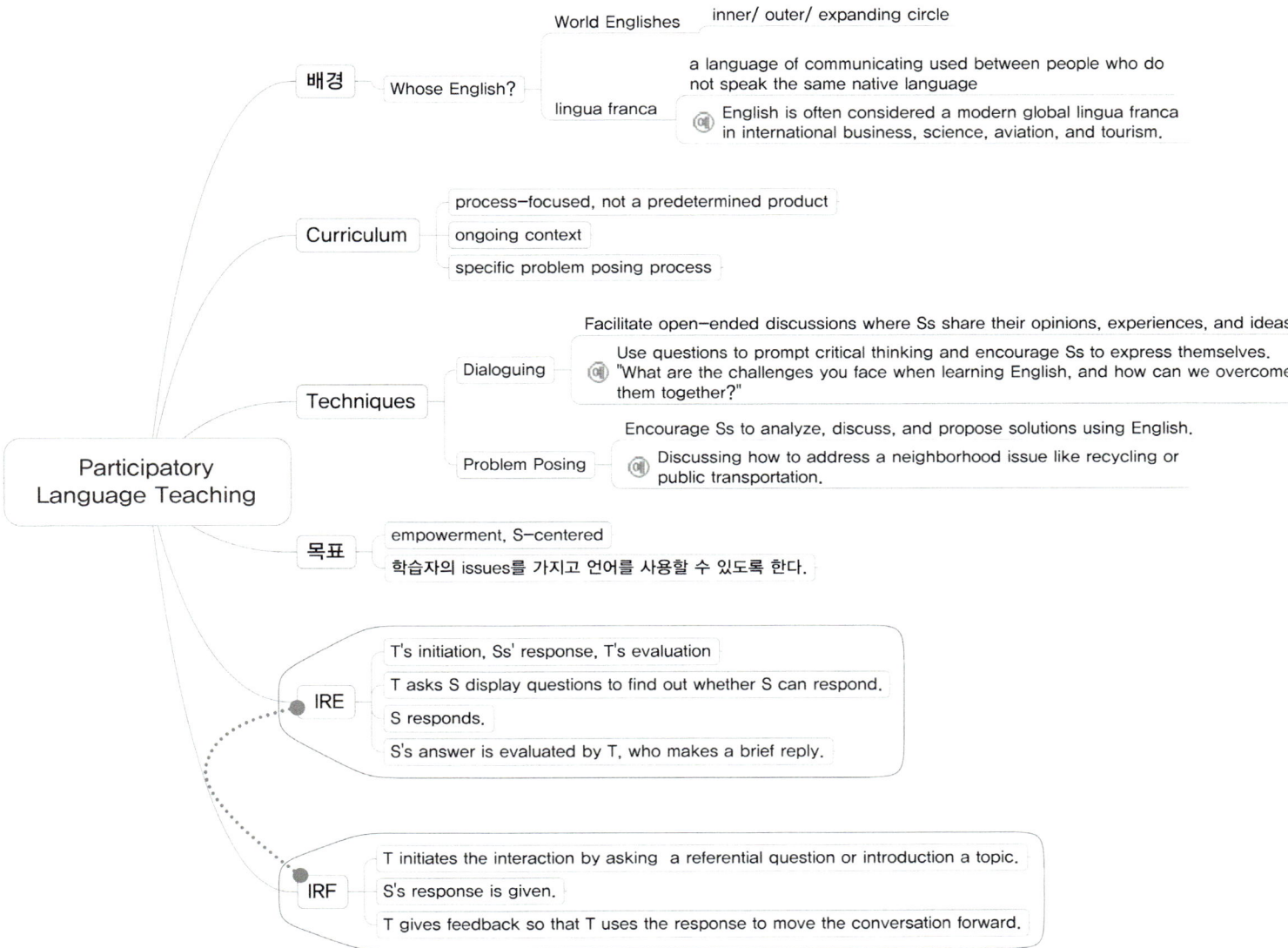

# 12 경험언어 교수법

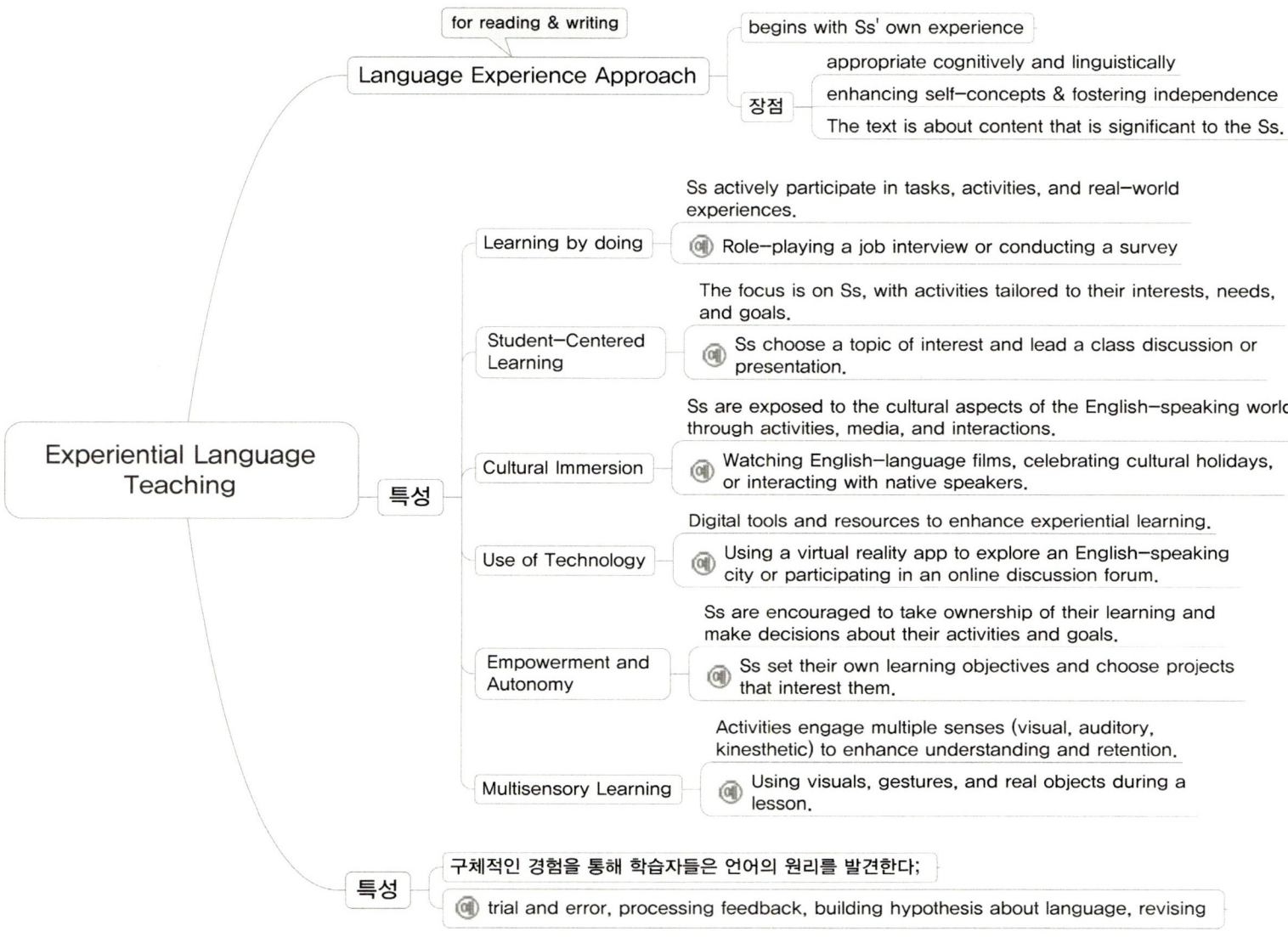

# 13 어휘중심 교수법

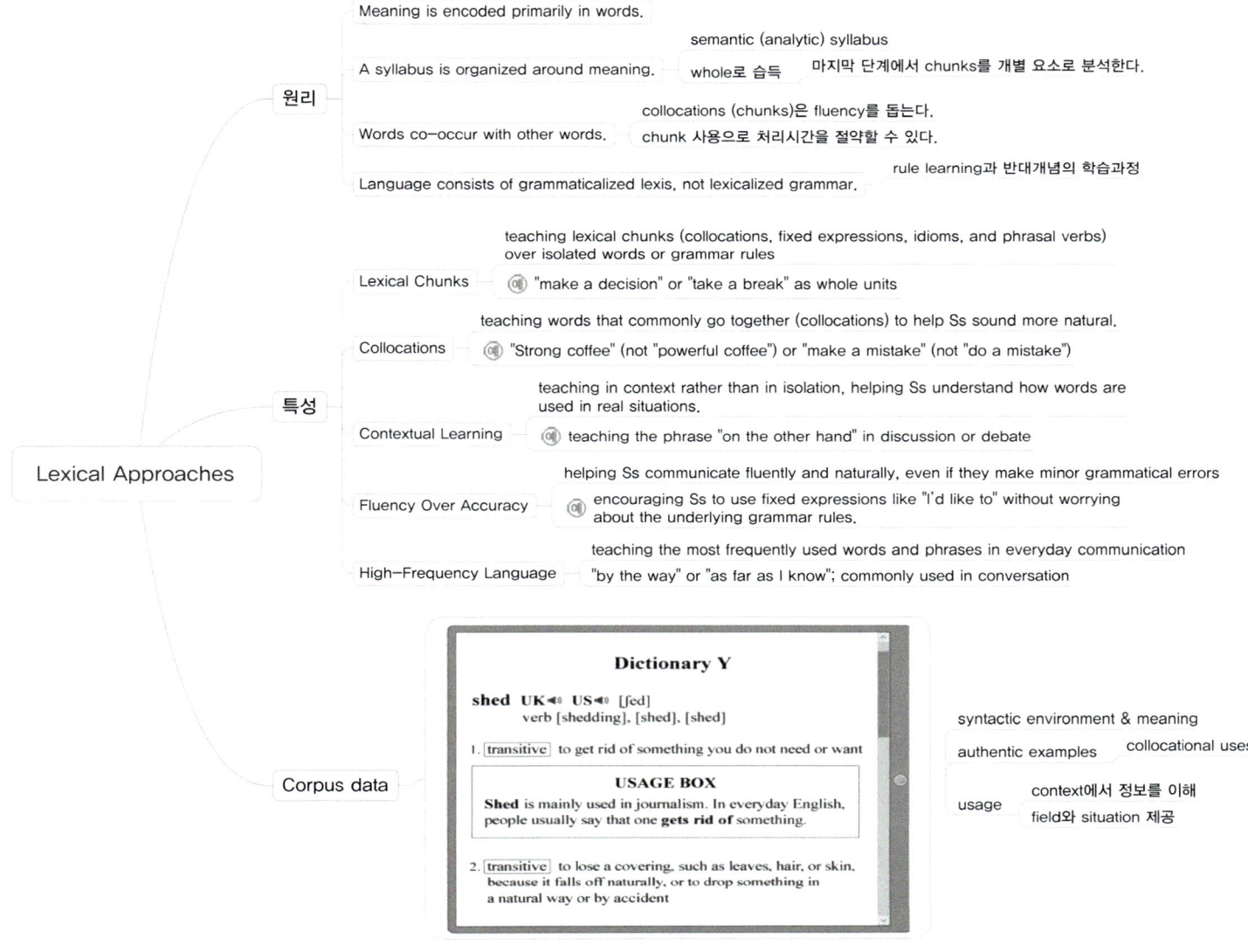

# 14 Focus on Form

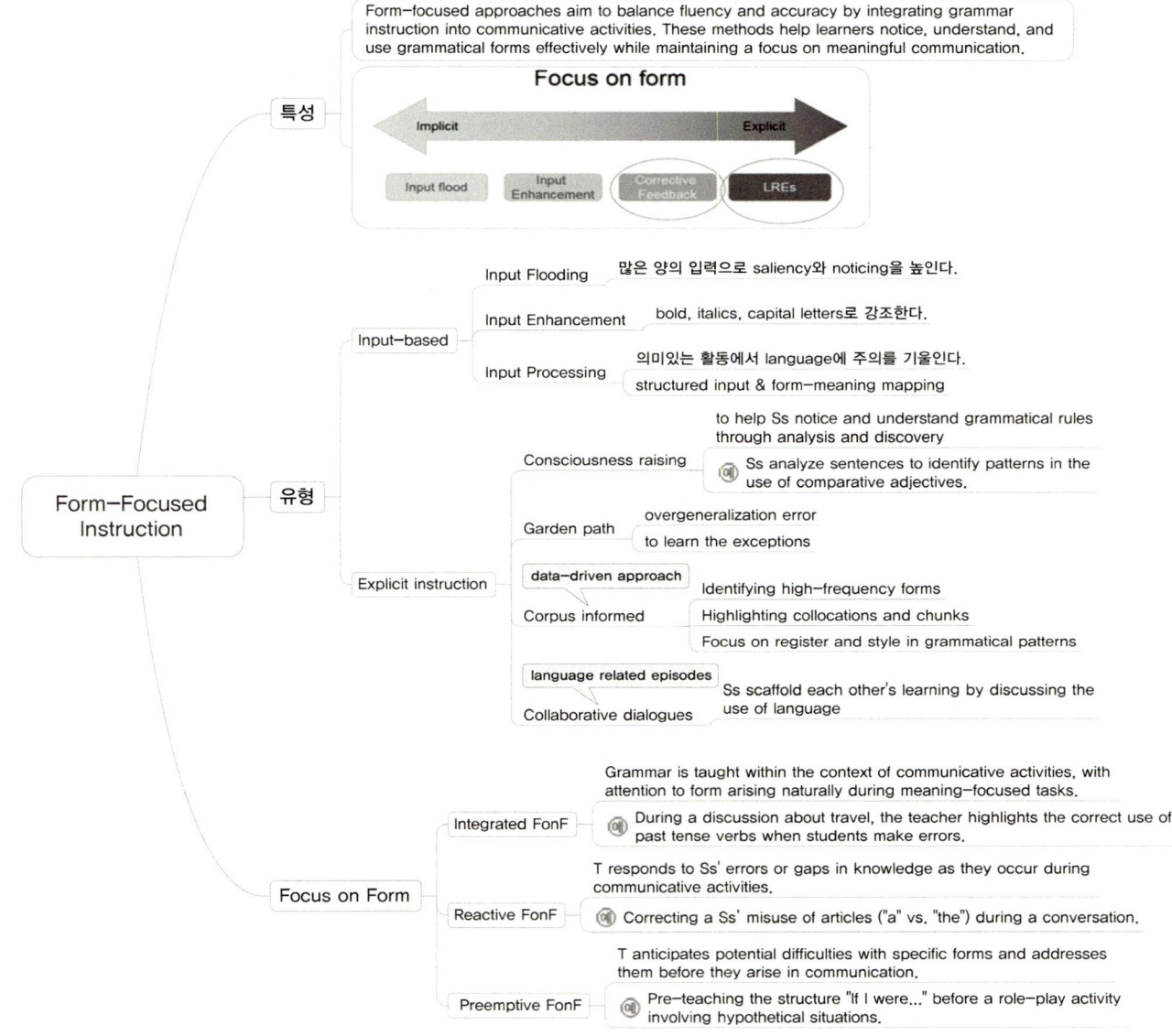

- **특성**: Form-focused approaches aim to balance fluency and accuracy by integrating grammar instruction into communicative activities. These methods help learners notice, understand, and use grammatical forms effectively while maintaining a focus on meaningful communication.

  **Focus on form**
  Implicit ← → Explicit
  Input flood | Input Enhancement | Corrective Feedback | LREs

- **Form-Focused Instruction**
  - **유형**
    - **Input-based**
      - Input Flooding — 많은 양의 입력으로 saliency와 noticing을 높인다.
      - Input Enhancement — bold, italics, capital letters로 강조한다.
      - Input Processing — 의미있는 활동에서 language에 주의를 기울인다. structured input & form-meaning mapping
    - **Explicit instruction**
      - Consciousness raising — to help Ss notice and understand grammatical rules through analysis and discovery
        - 예) Ss analyze sentences to identify patterns in the use of comparative adjectives.
      - Garden path — overgeneralization error / to learn the exceptions
      - Corpus informed [data-driven approach]
        - Identifying high-frequency forms
        - Highlighting collocations and chunks
        - Focus on register and style in grammatical patterns
      - Collaborative dialogues [language related episodes] — Ss scaffold each other's learning by discussing the use of language

- **Focus on Form**
  - Integrated FonF — Grammar is taught within the context of communicative activities, with attention to form arising naturally during meaning-focused tasks.
    - 예) During a discussion about travel, the teacher highlights the correct use of past tense verbs when students make errors.
  - Reactive FonF — T responds to Ss' errors or gaps in knowledge as they occur during communicative activities.
    - 예) Correcting a Ss' misuse of articles ("a" vs. "the") during a conversation.
  - Preemptive FonF — T anticipates potential difficulties with specific forms and addresses them before they arise in communication.
    - 예) Pre-teaching the structure "If I were..." before a role-play activity involving hypothetical situations.

권영주 영어교육론 MIND MAP

# 05.
# English Assessment

# MEMO

권영주 영어교육론 MIND MAP

# 01 언어 평가

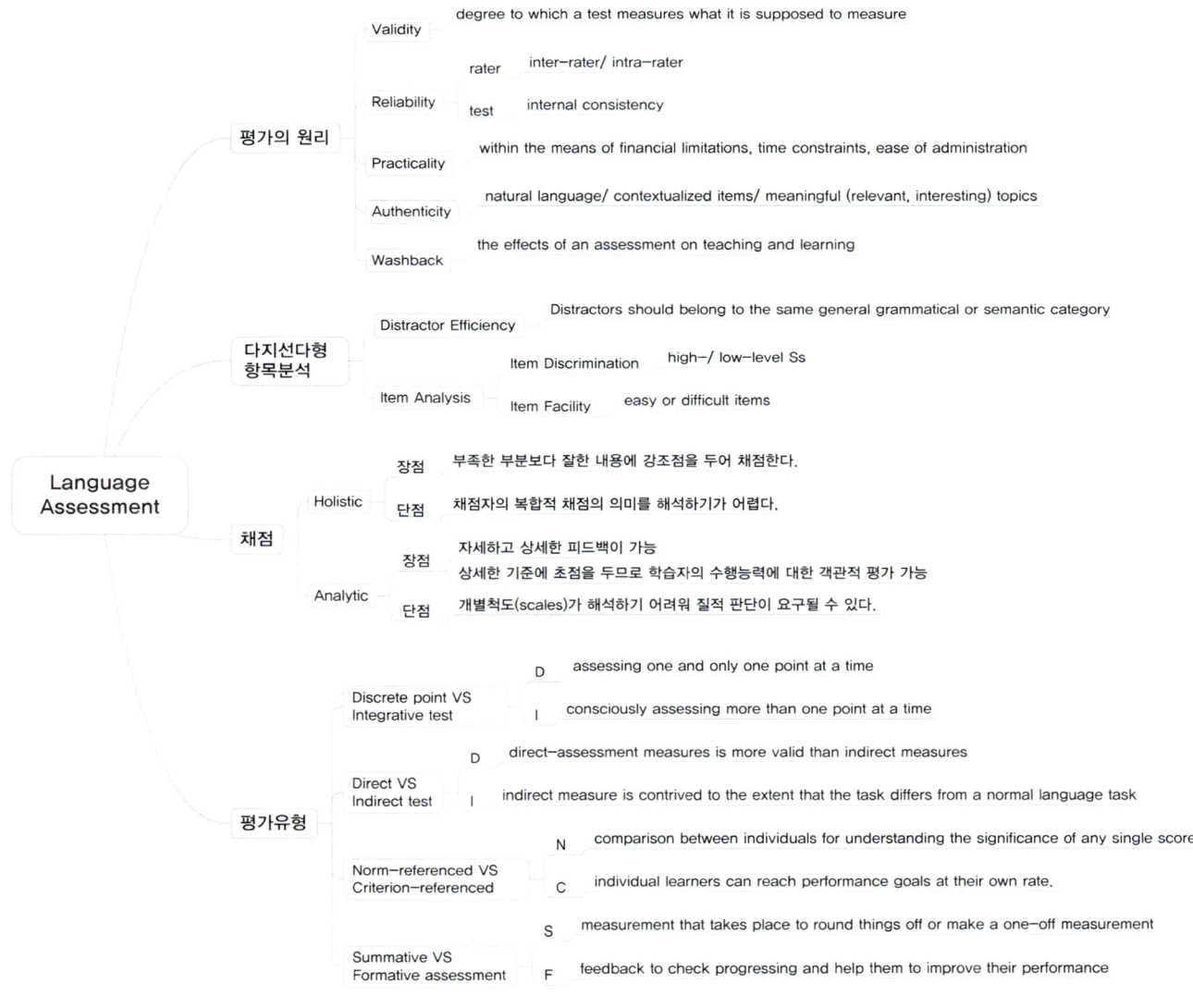

# 02 평가 원리 (1)

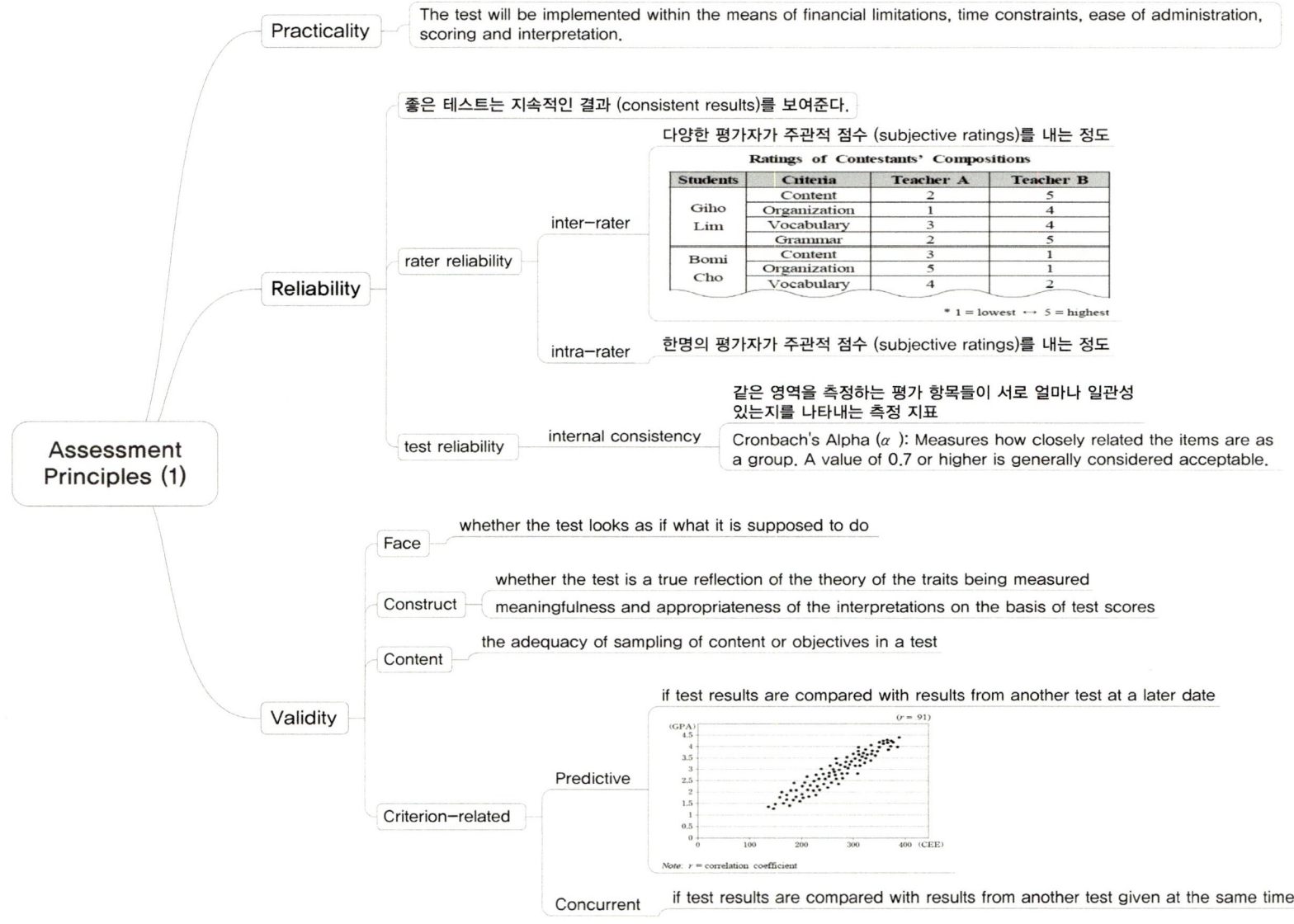

**Assessment Principles (1)**

- **Practicality**: The test will be implemented within the means of financial limitations, time constraints, ease of administration, scoring and interpretation.

- **Reliability**: 좋은 테스트는 지속적인 결과 (consistent results)를 보여준다.
  - **rater reliability**
    - **inter-rater**: 다양한 평가자가 주관적 점수 (subjective ratings)를 내는 정도
    
      Ratings of Contestants' Compositions
      
      | Students | Criteria | Teacher A | Teacher B |
      |---|---|---|---|
      | Giho Lim | Content | 2 | 5 |
      |  | Organization | 1 | 4 |
      |  | Vocabulary | 3 | 4 |
      |  | Grammar | 2 | 5 |
      | Bomi Cho | Content | 3 | 1 |
      |  | Organization | 5 | 1 |
      |  | Vocabulary | 4 | 2 |
      
      * 1 = lowest ↔ 5 = highest
    - **intra-rater**: 한명의 평가자가 주관적 점수 (subjective ratings)를 내는 정도
  - **test reliability**
    - **internal consistency**: 같은 영역을 측정하는 평가 항목들이 서로 얼마나 일관성 있는지를 나타내는 측정 지표
    
      Cronbach's Alpha ($\alpha$): Measures how closely related the items are as a group. A value of 0.7 or higher is generally considered acceptable.

- **Validity**
  - **Face**: whether the test looks as if what it is supposed to do
  - **Construct**: whether the test is a true reflection of the theory of the traits being measured; meaningfulness and appropriateness of the interpretations on the basis of test scores
  - **Content**: the adequacy of sampling of content or objectives in a test
  - **Criterion-related**
    - **Predictive**: if test results are compared with results from another test at a later date
    - **Concurrent**: if test results are compared with results from another test given at the same time

# 03 평가 원리 (2)

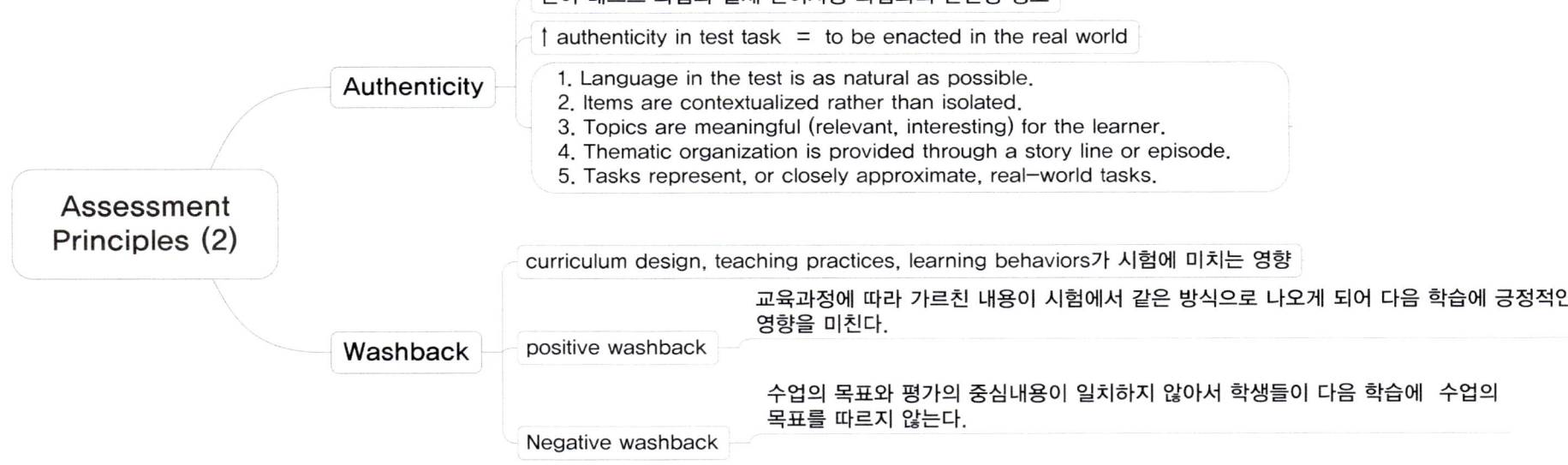

# 04 시험 유형 (1)

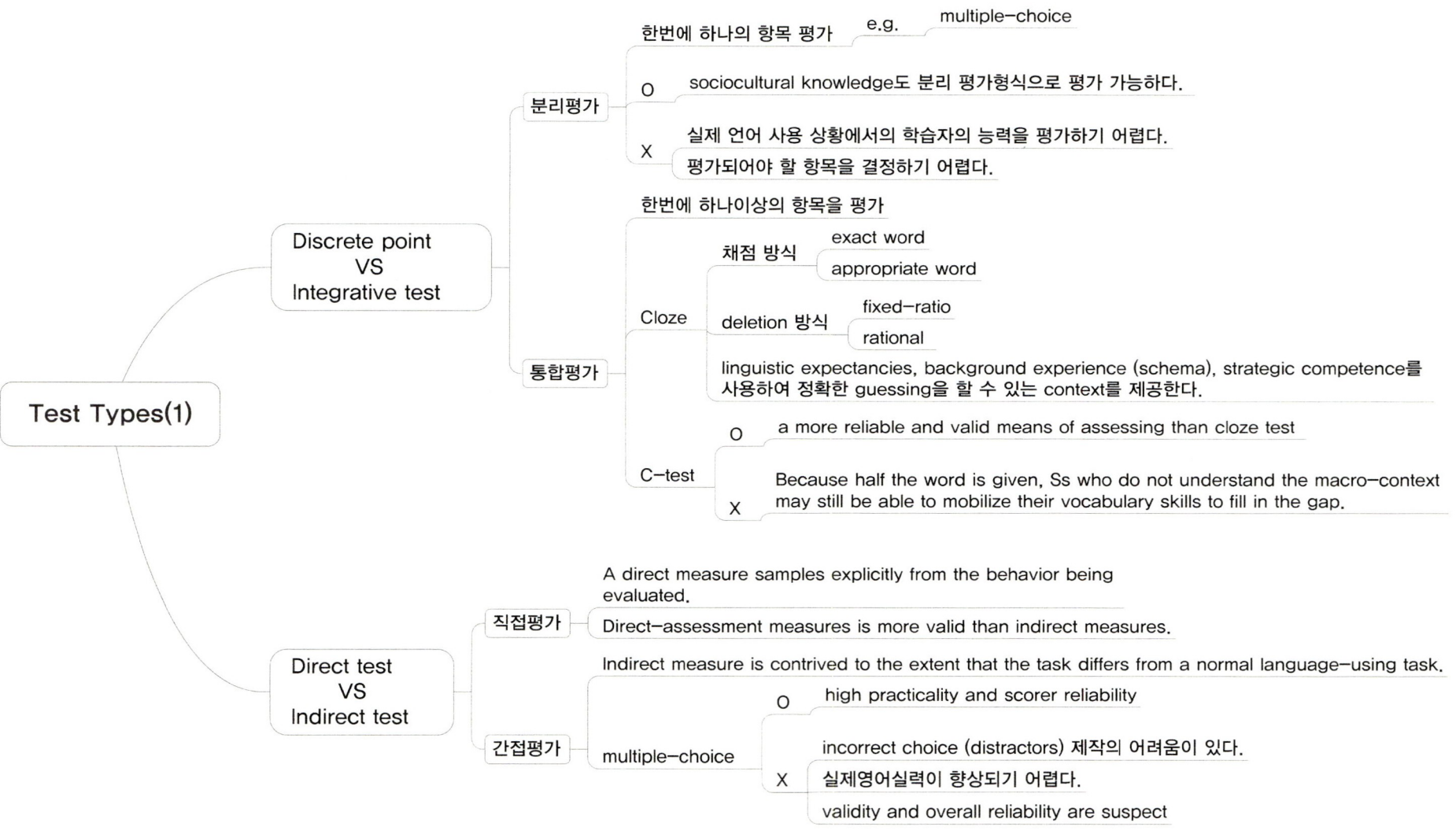

# 05 시험 유형 (2)

권영주 영어교육론 MIND MAP

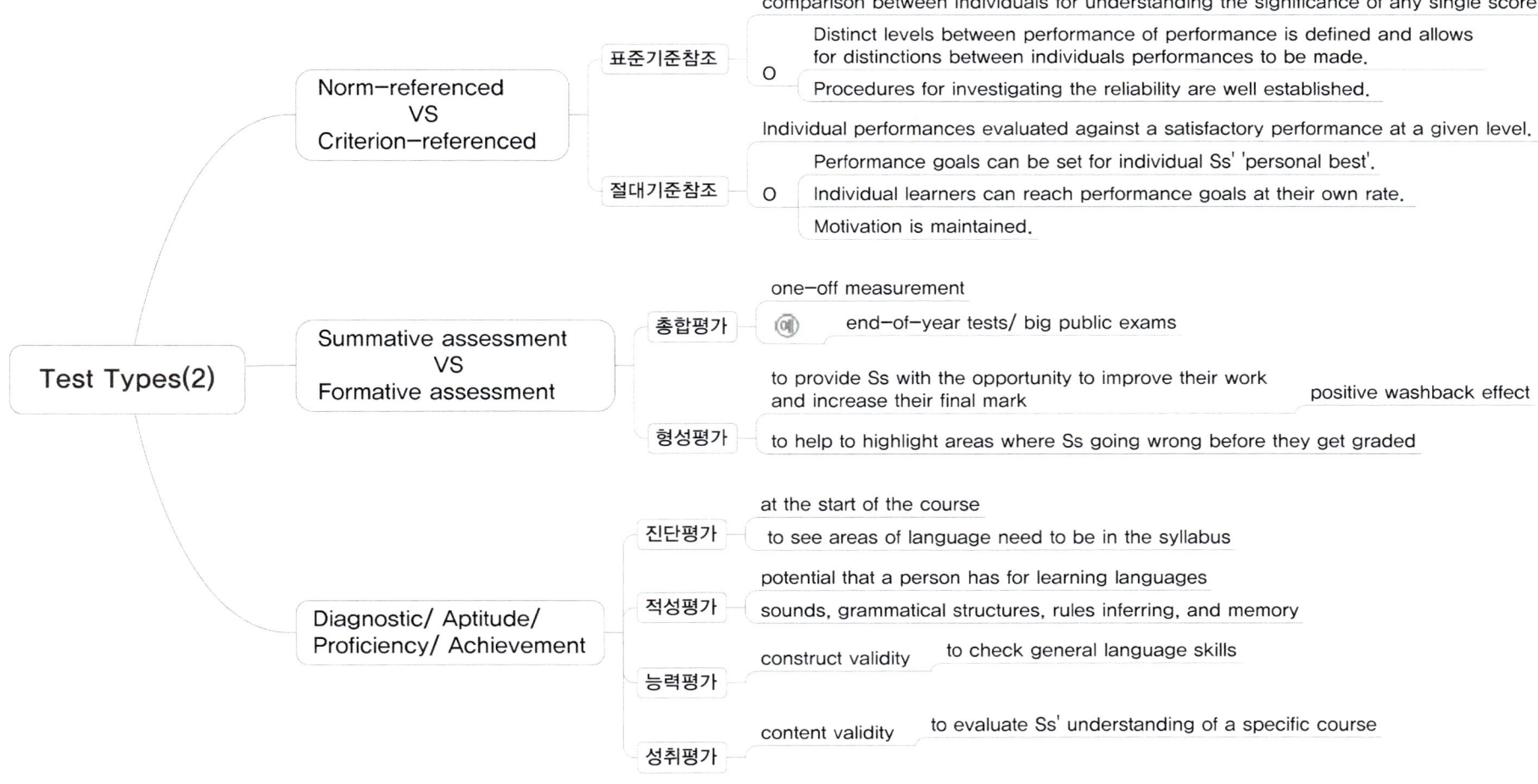

05 English Assessment

# 06 대체 평가 (1)

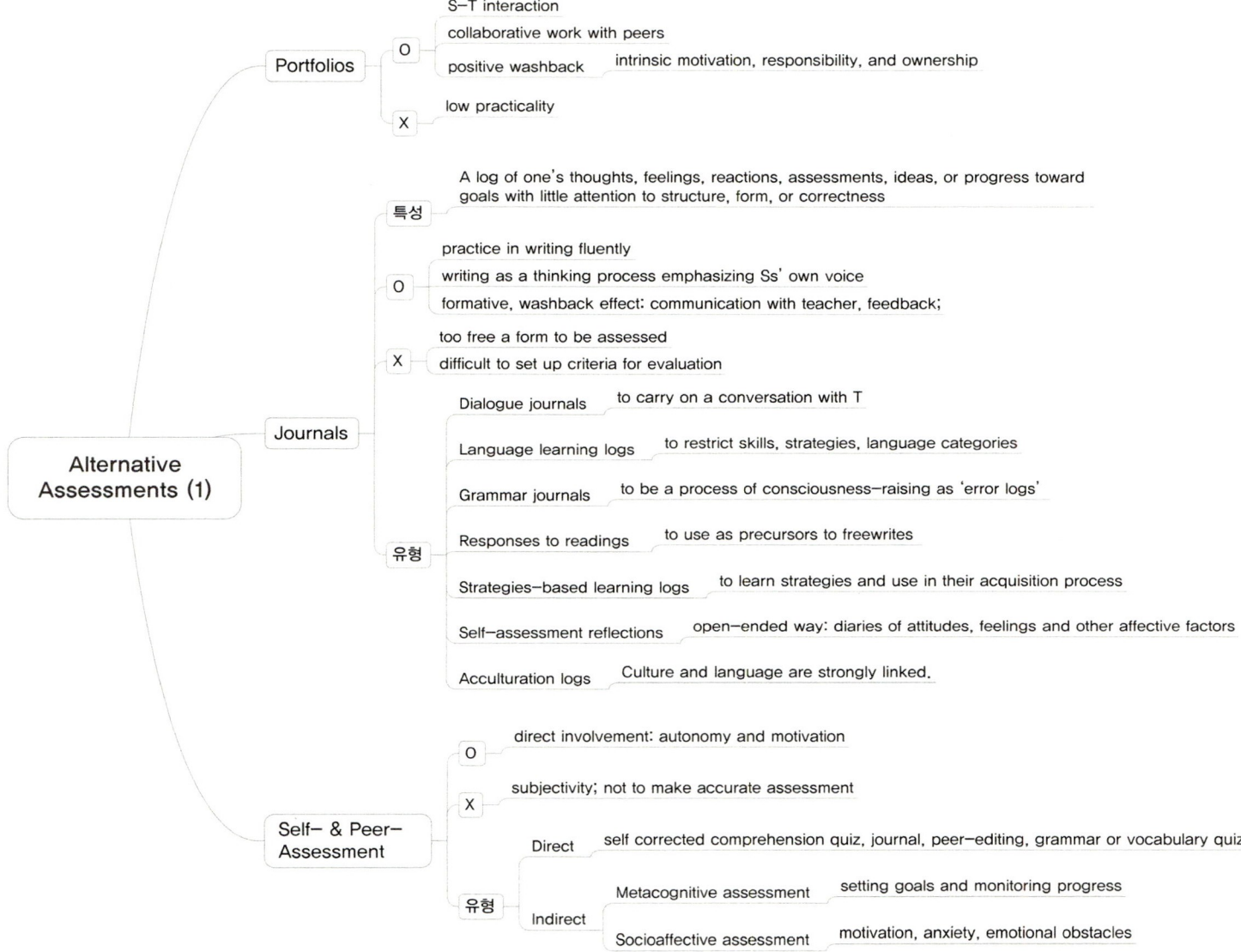

# 07 대체 평가 (2)

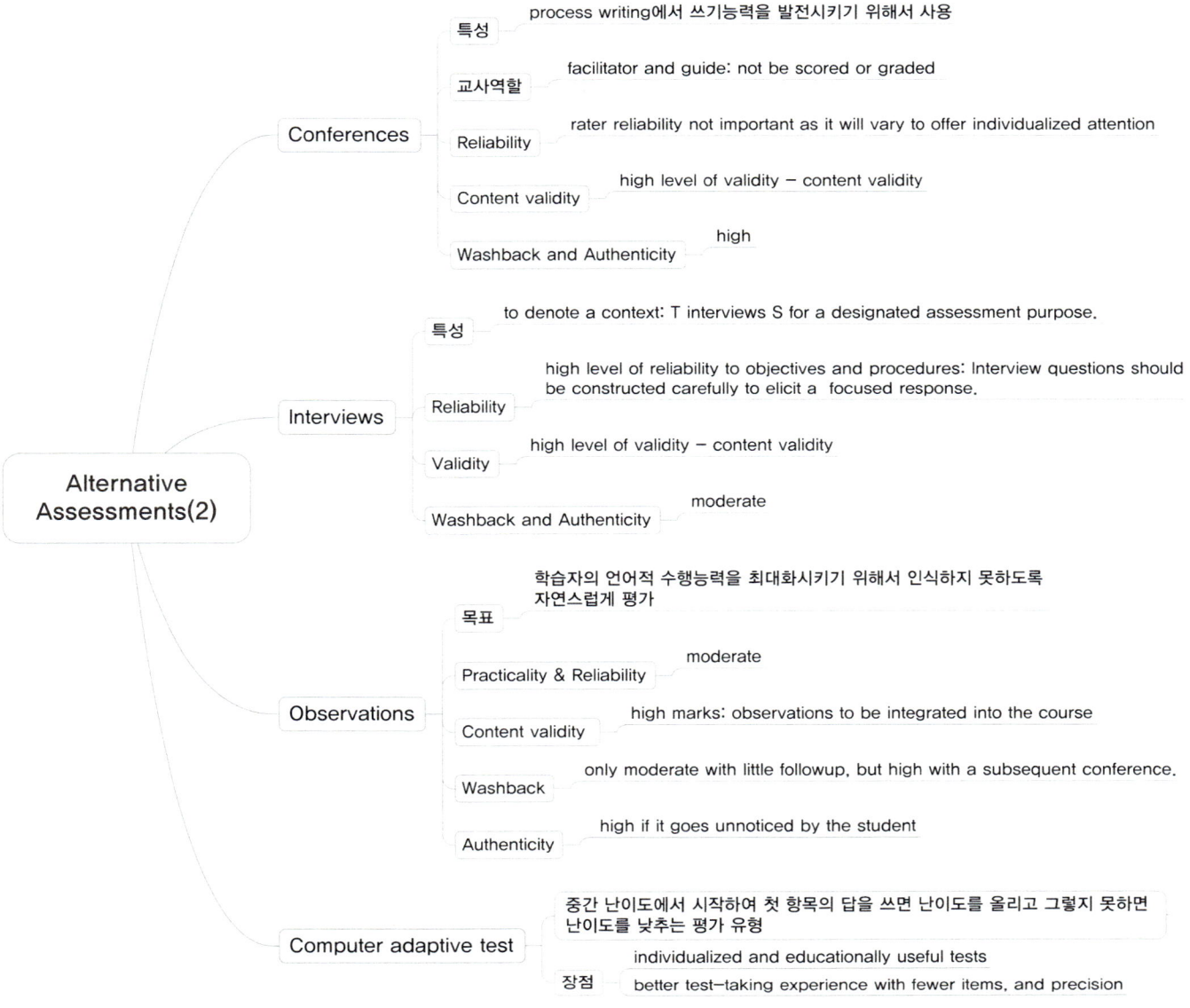

# 08 시험항목 분석

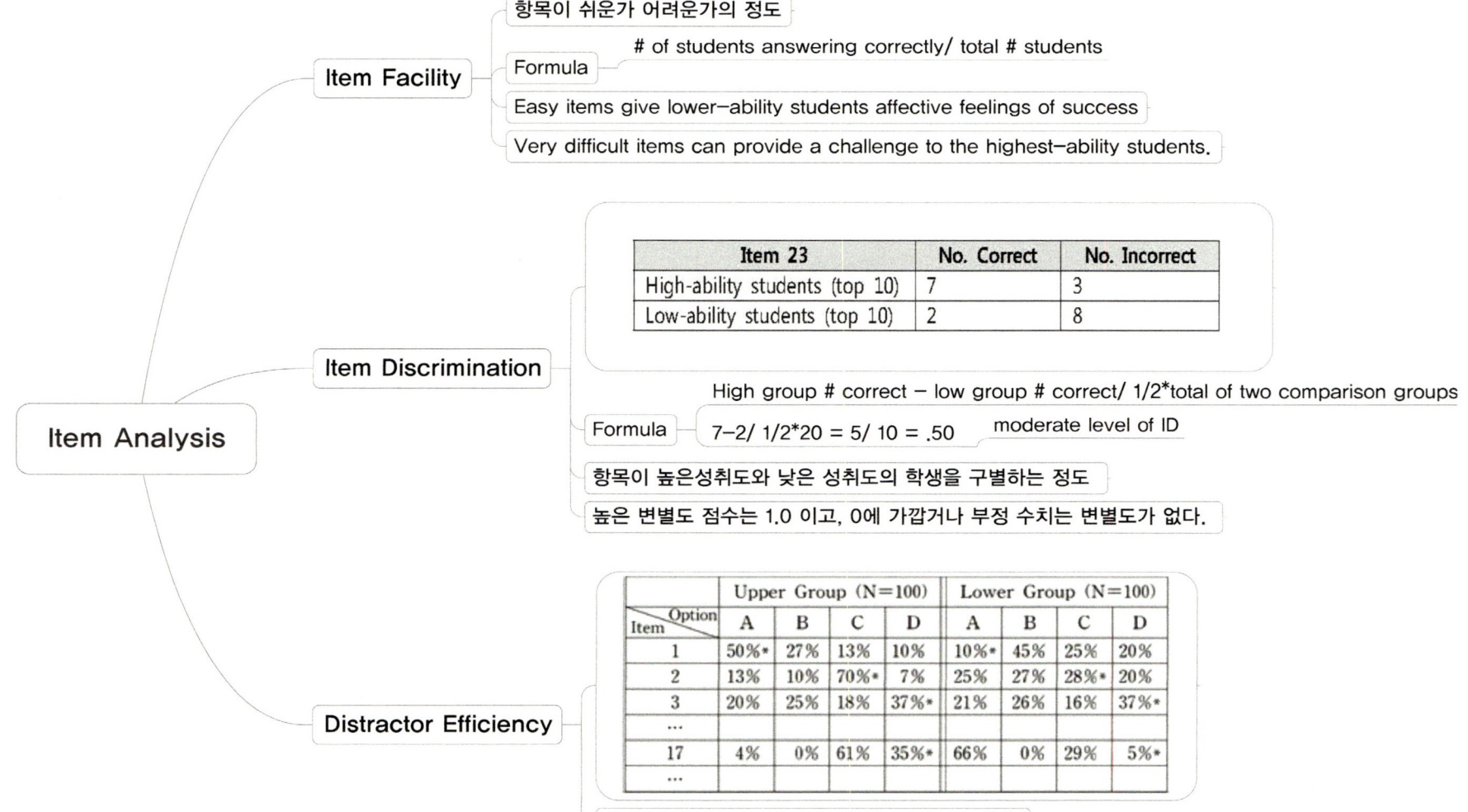

# 06. Teaching Listening

권영주 영어교육론 MIND MAP

# MEMO

# 01 듣기 지도

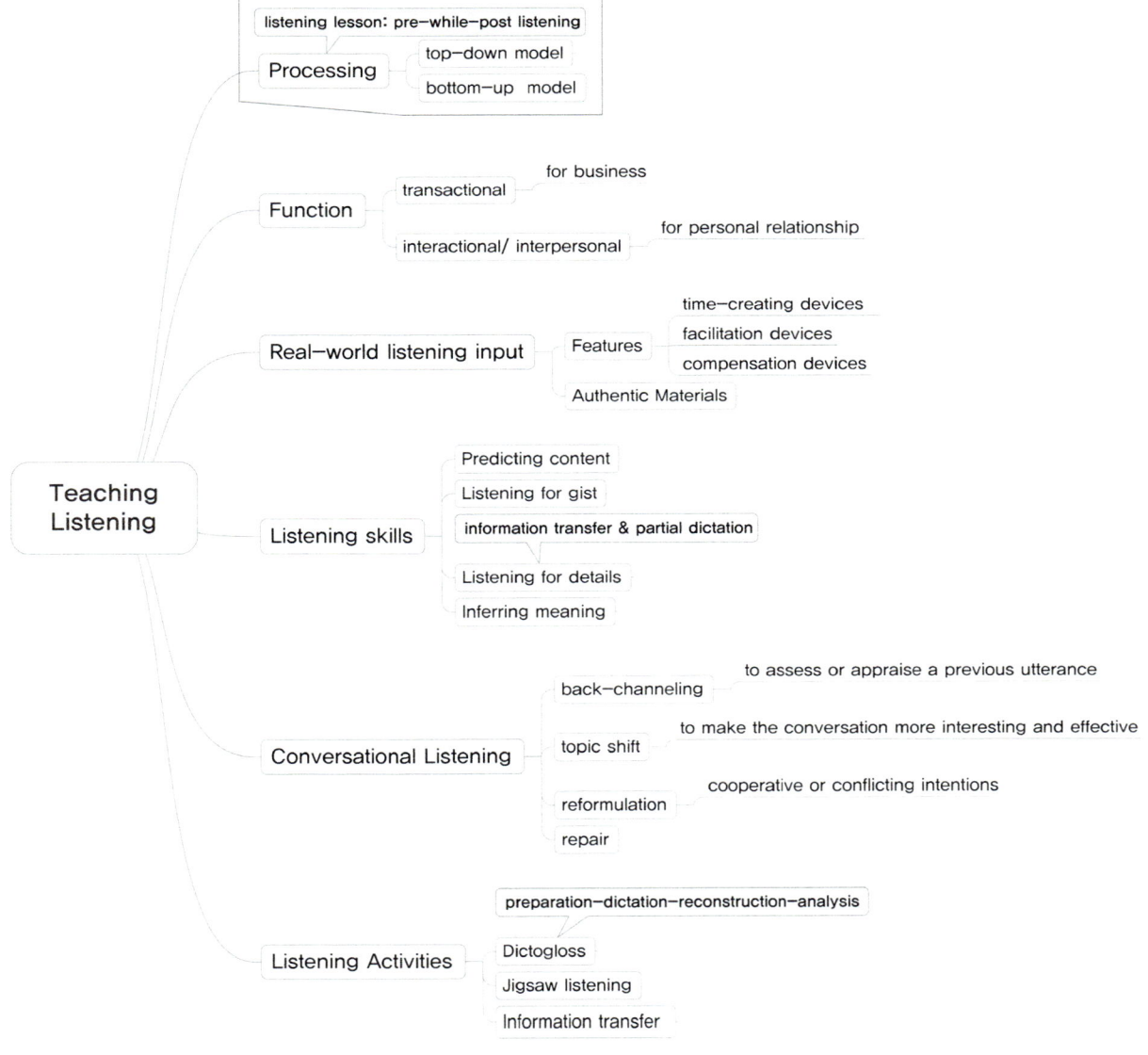

## 02 듣기 언어의 기능

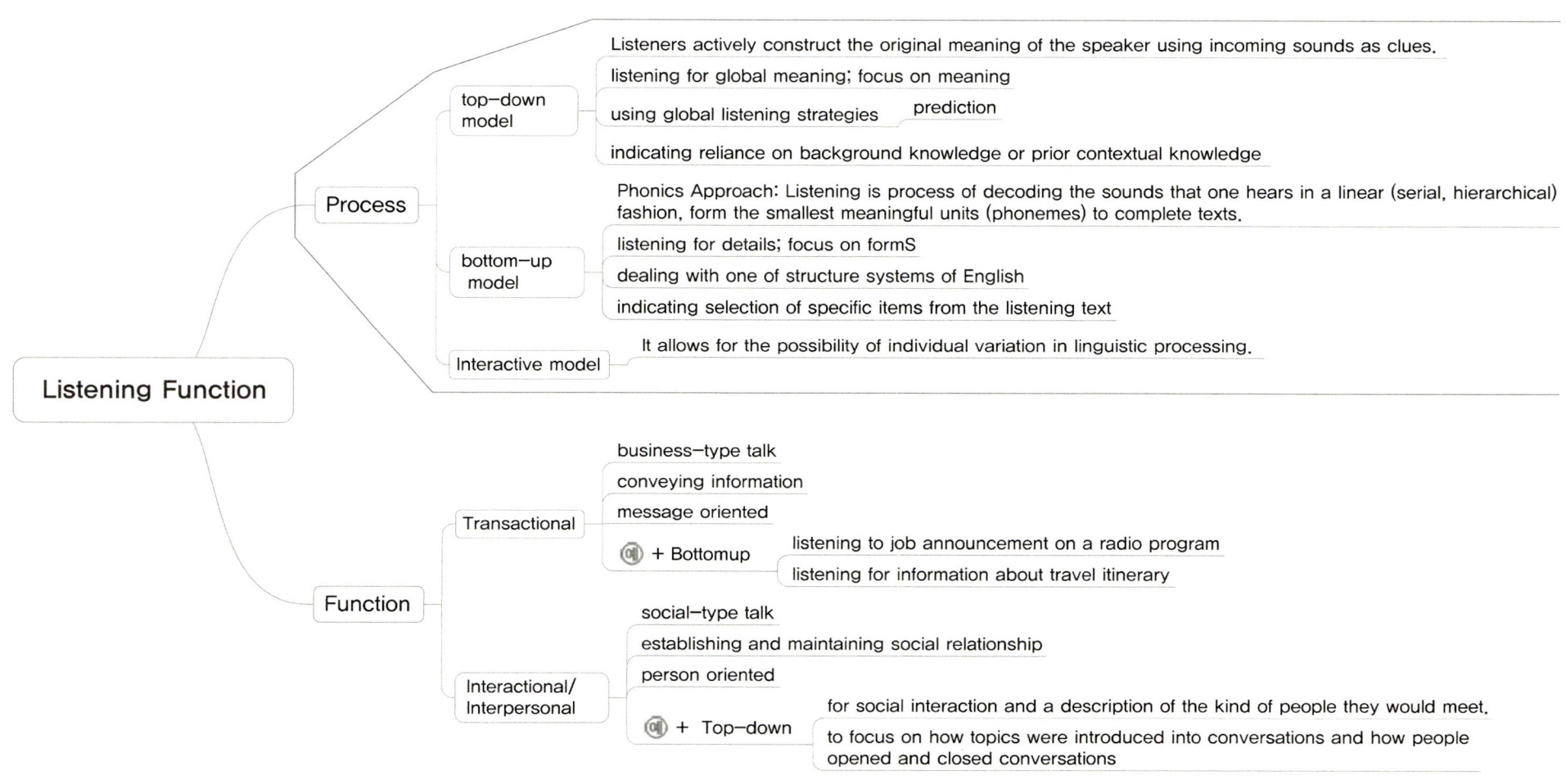

## 03 듣기 자료

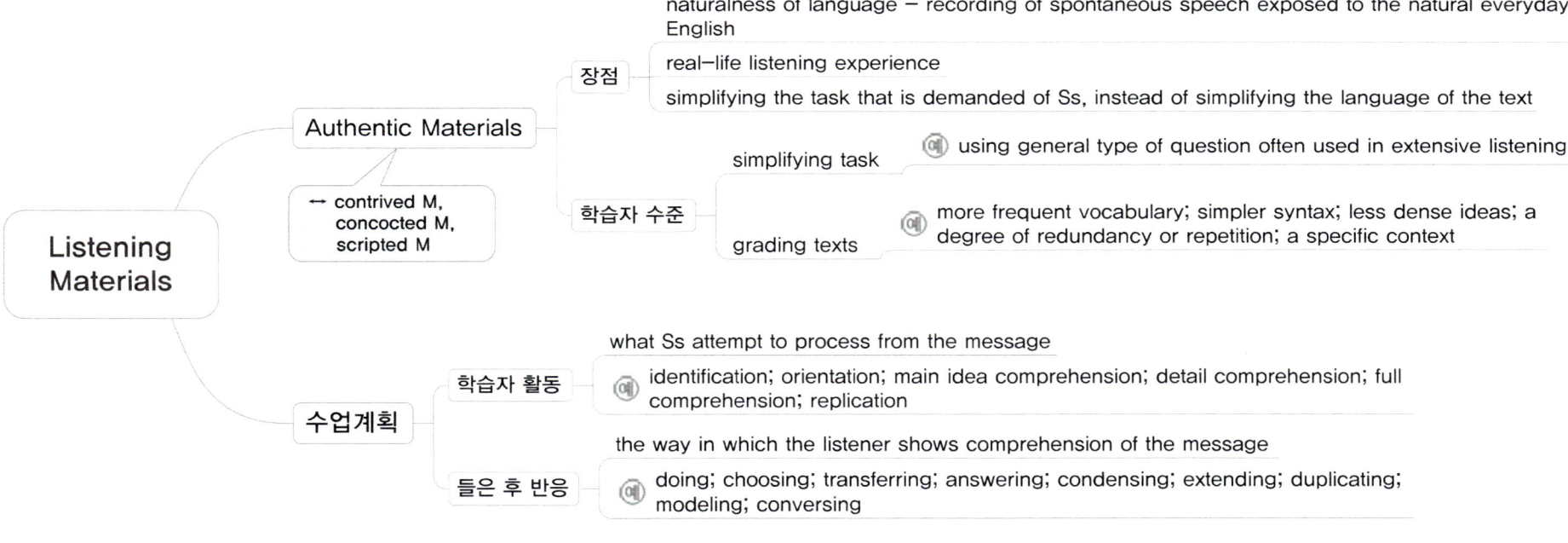

- **Listening Materials**
  - **Authentic Materials** ↔ contrived M, concocted M, scripted M
    - 장점
      - naturalness of language – recording of spontaneous speech exposed to the natural everyday English
      - real-life listening experience
      - simplifying the task that is demanded of Ss, instead of simplifying the language of the text
    - 학습자 수준
      - simplifying task — 예) using general type of question often used in extensive listening
      - grading texts — 예) more frequent vocabulary; simpler syntax; less dense ideas; a degree of redundancy or repetition; a specific context
  - 수업계획
    - 학습자 활동: what Ss attempt to process from the message
      - 예) identification; orientation; main idea comprehension; detail comprehension; full comprehension; replication
    - 들은 후 반응: the way in which the listener shows comprehension of the message
      - 예) doing; choosing; transferring; answering; condensing; extending; duplicating; modeling; conversing

## 04 듣기 수업형식

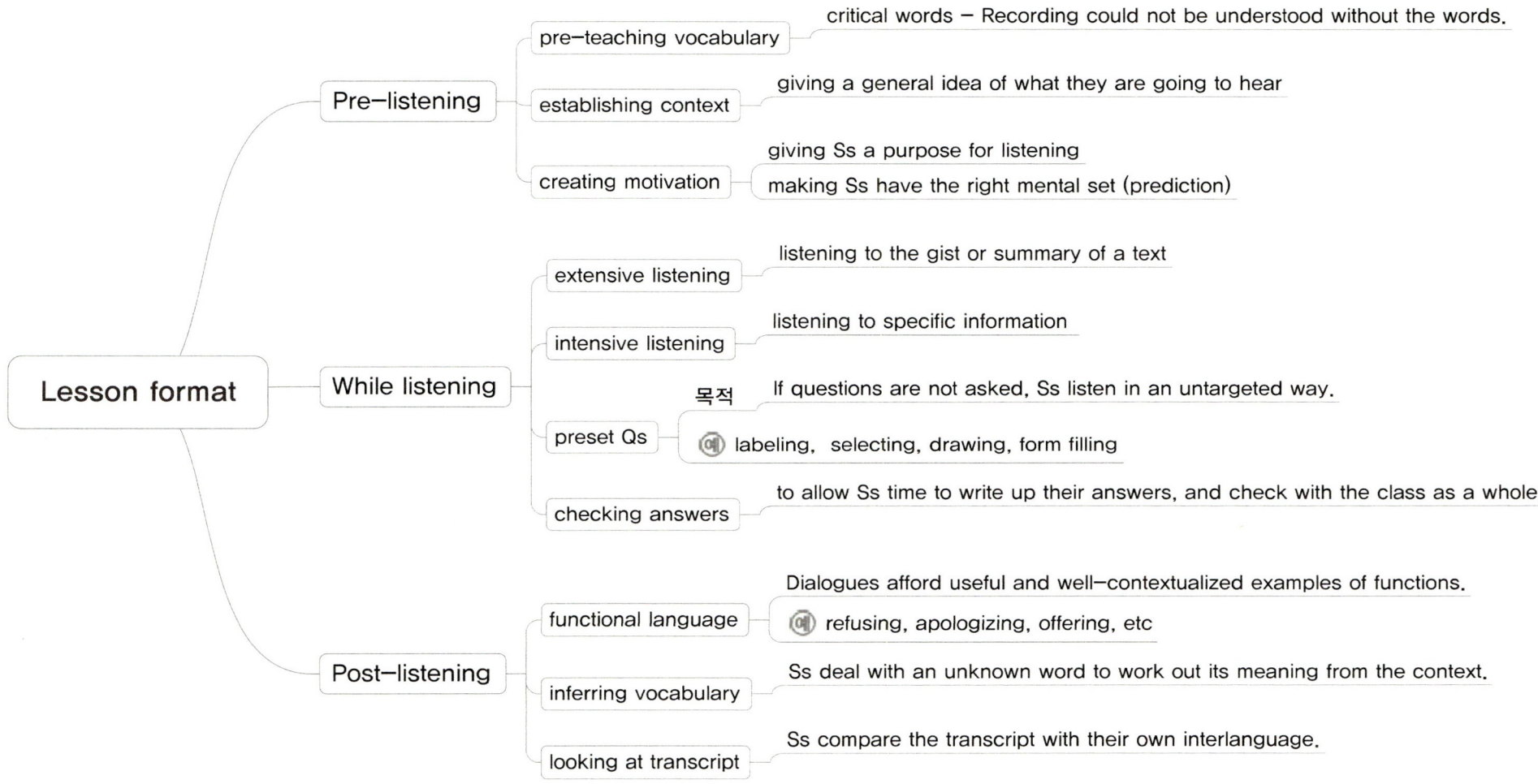

# 05 듣기 전략

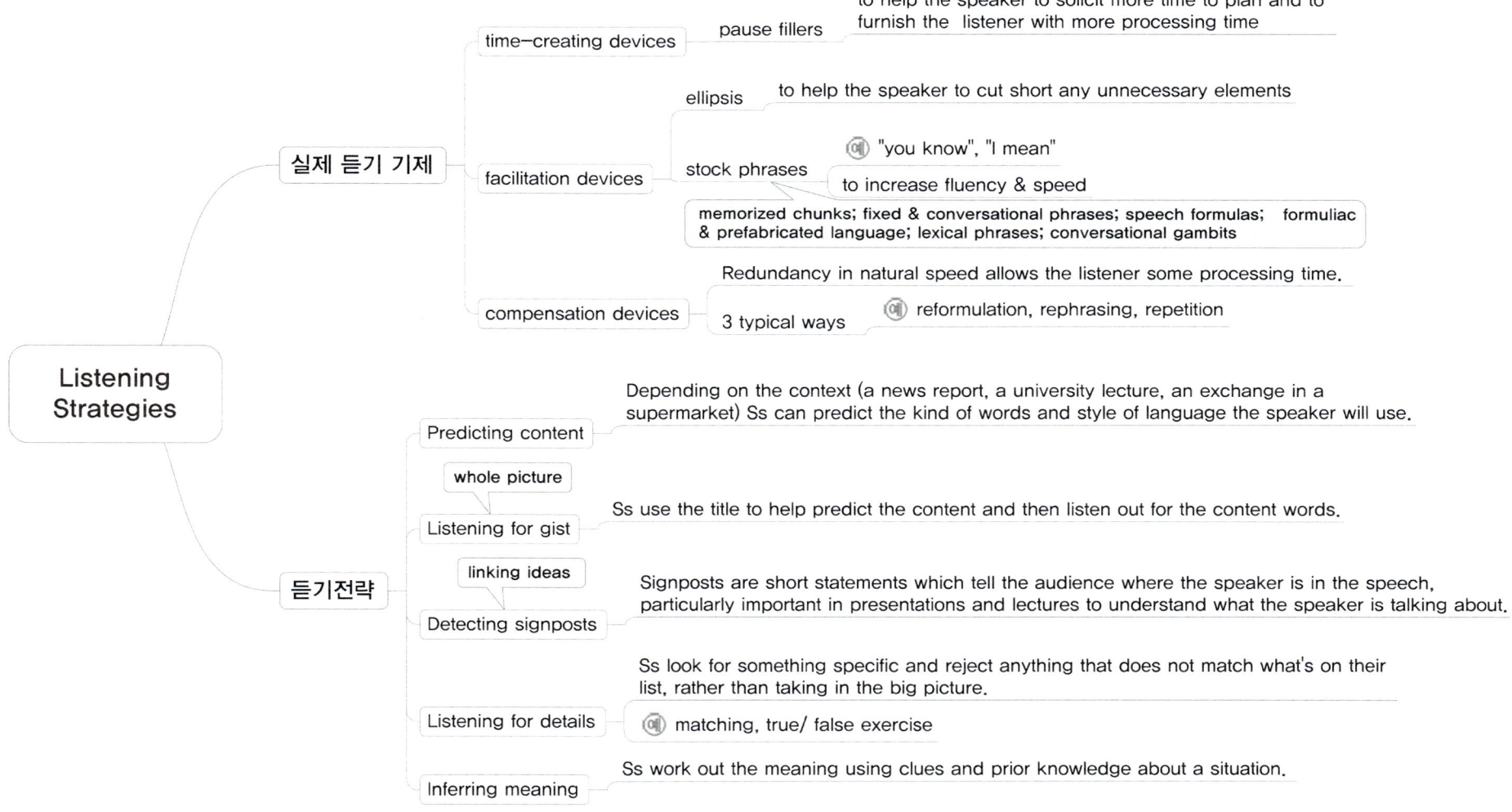

# 06 대화체 특성

# 07 듣기 활동

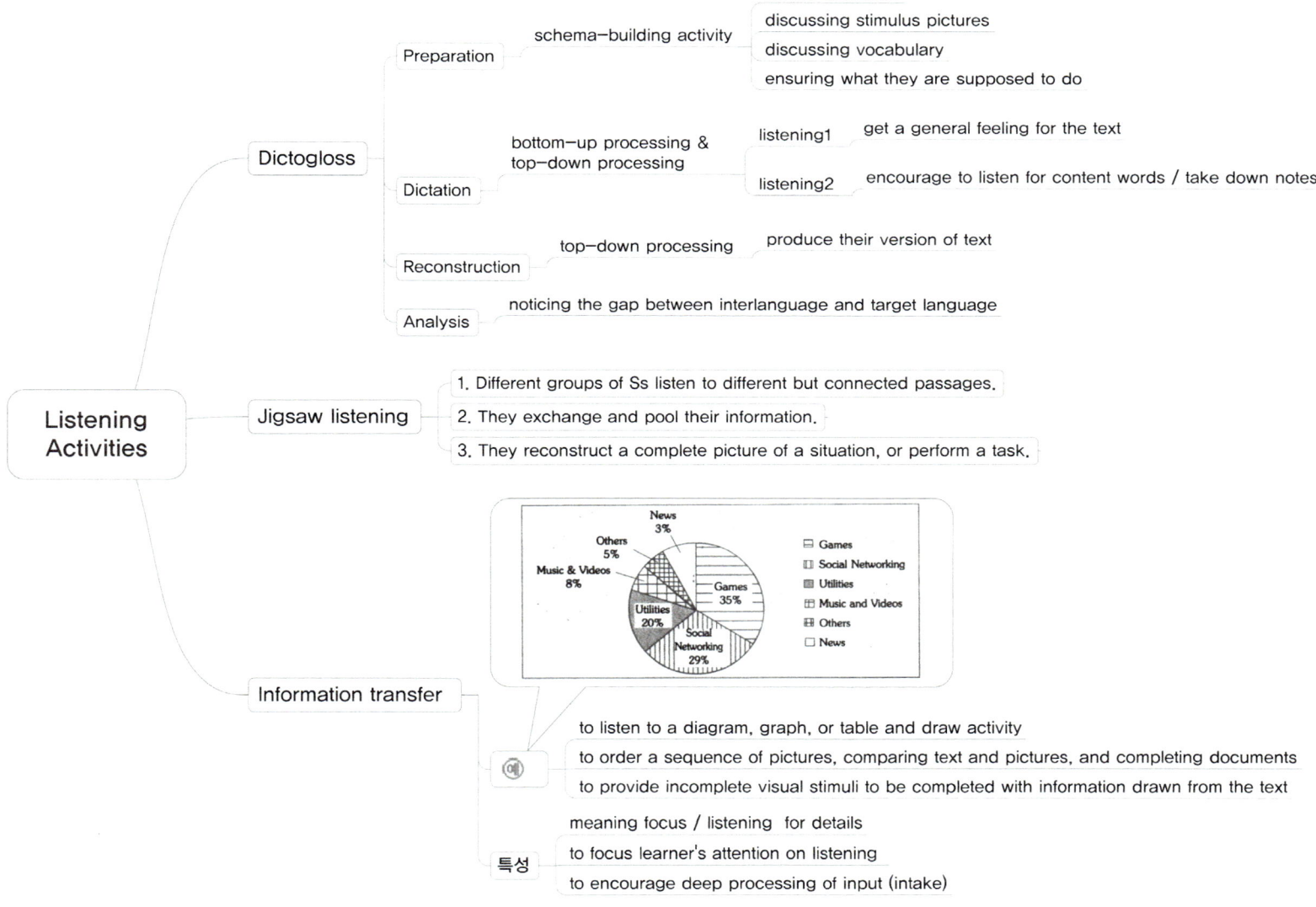

# MEMO

권영주 영어교육론 MIND MAP

# 07.
# Teaching Speaking

권영주 영어교육론 MIND MAP

# MEMO

# 01 말하기지도

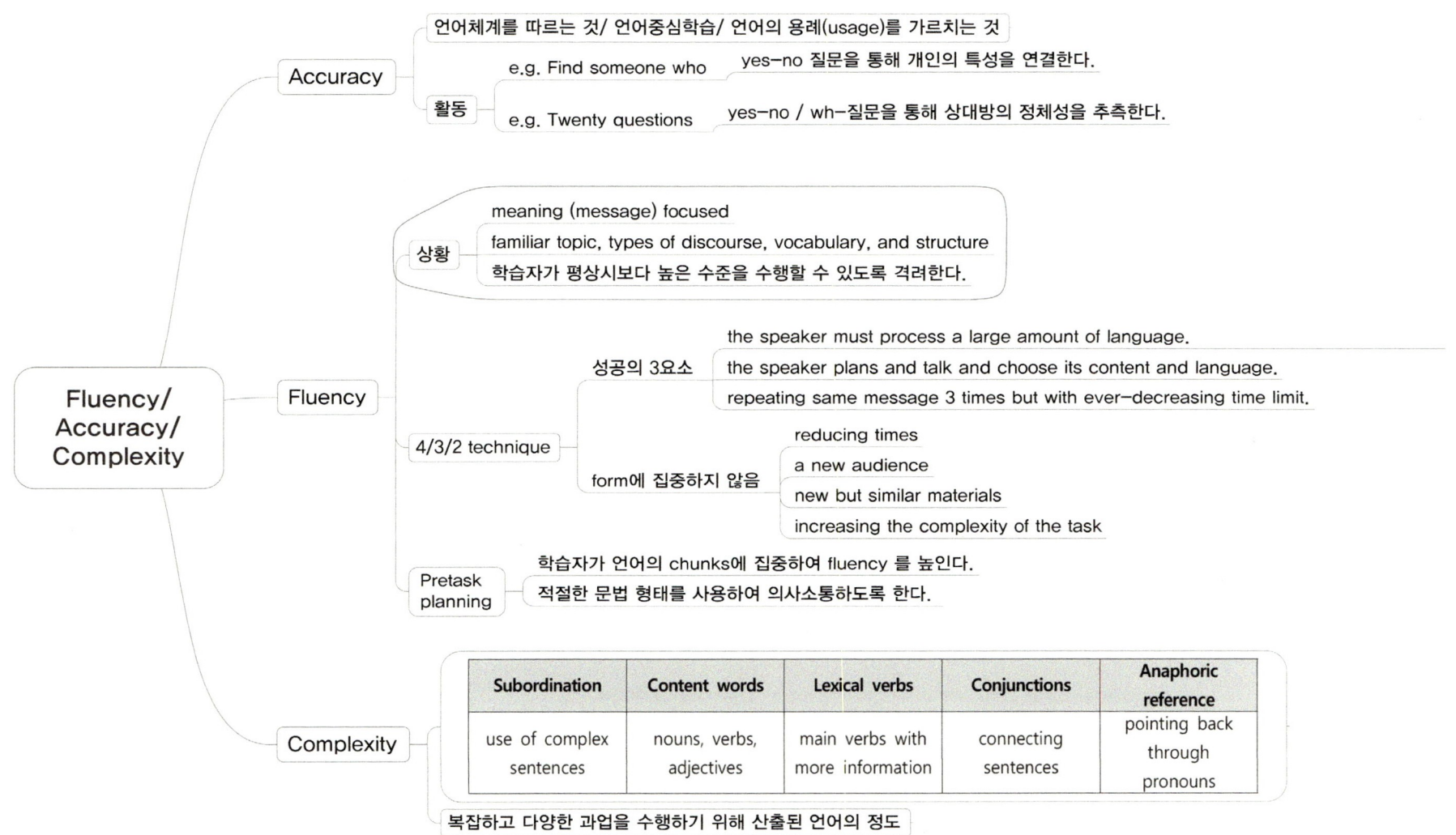

## 03 말하기 특성

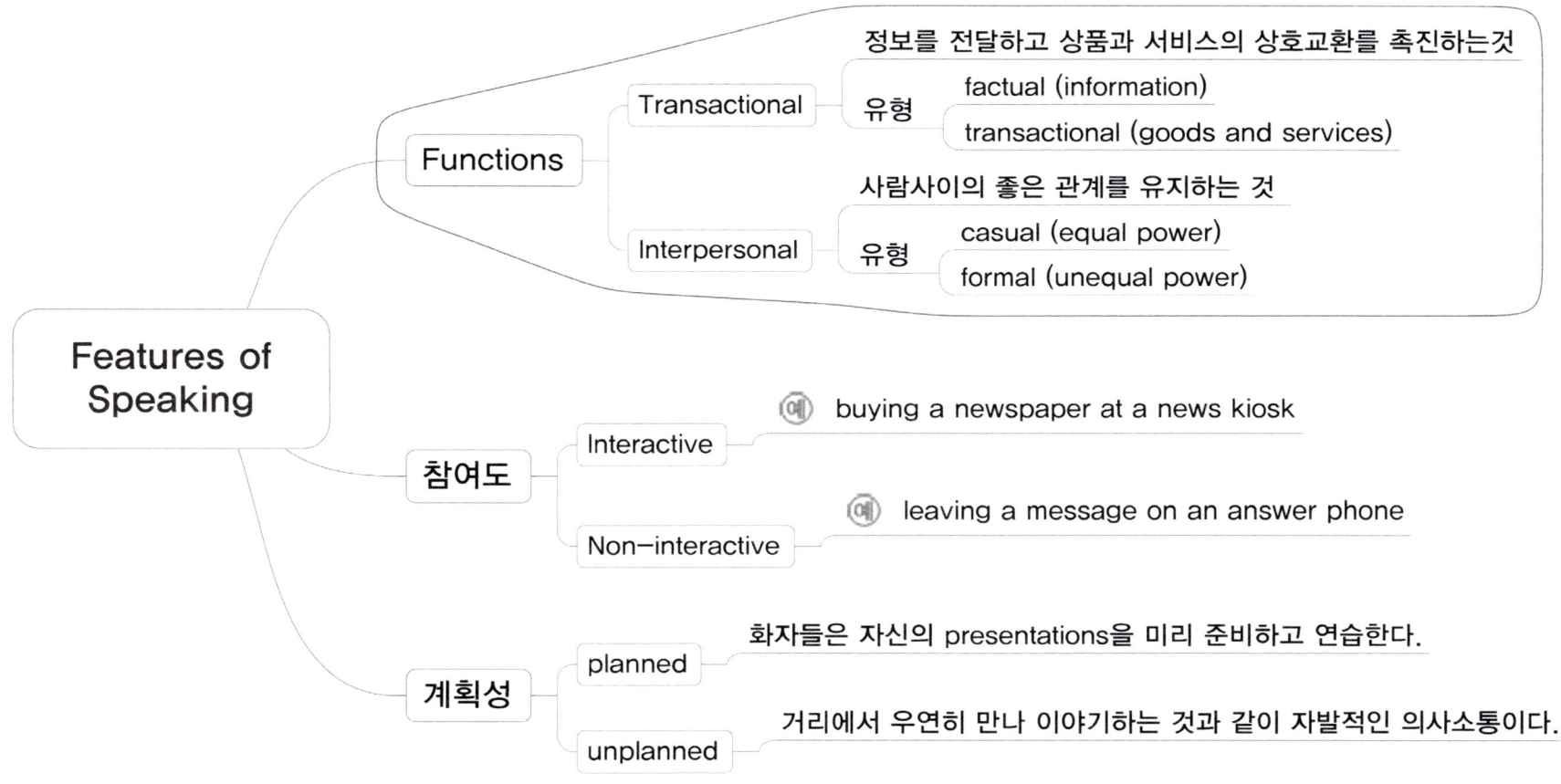

# 04 대화말하기 지도

## 05 대화체 기제

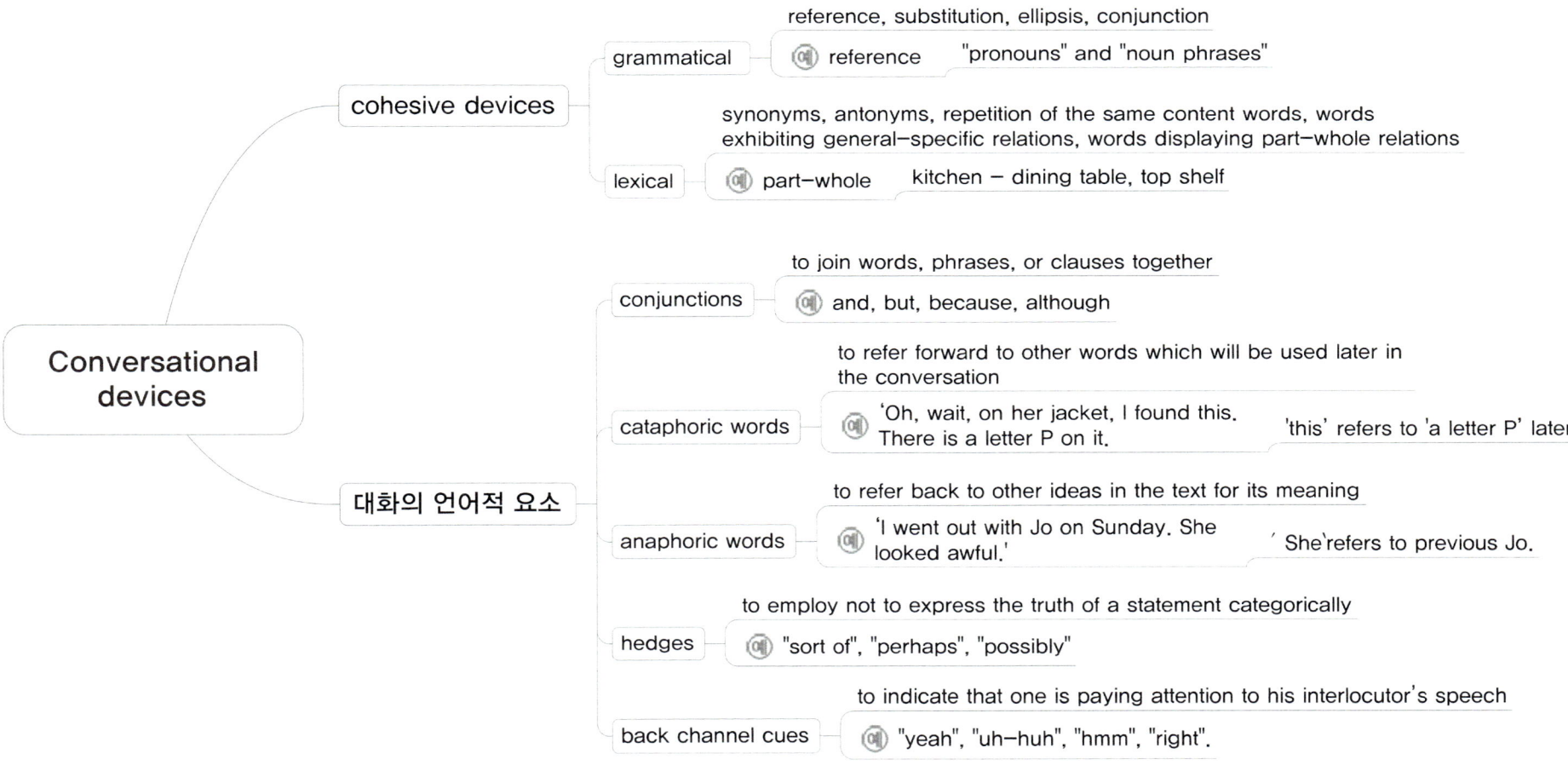

# 07 말하기 활동 (1)

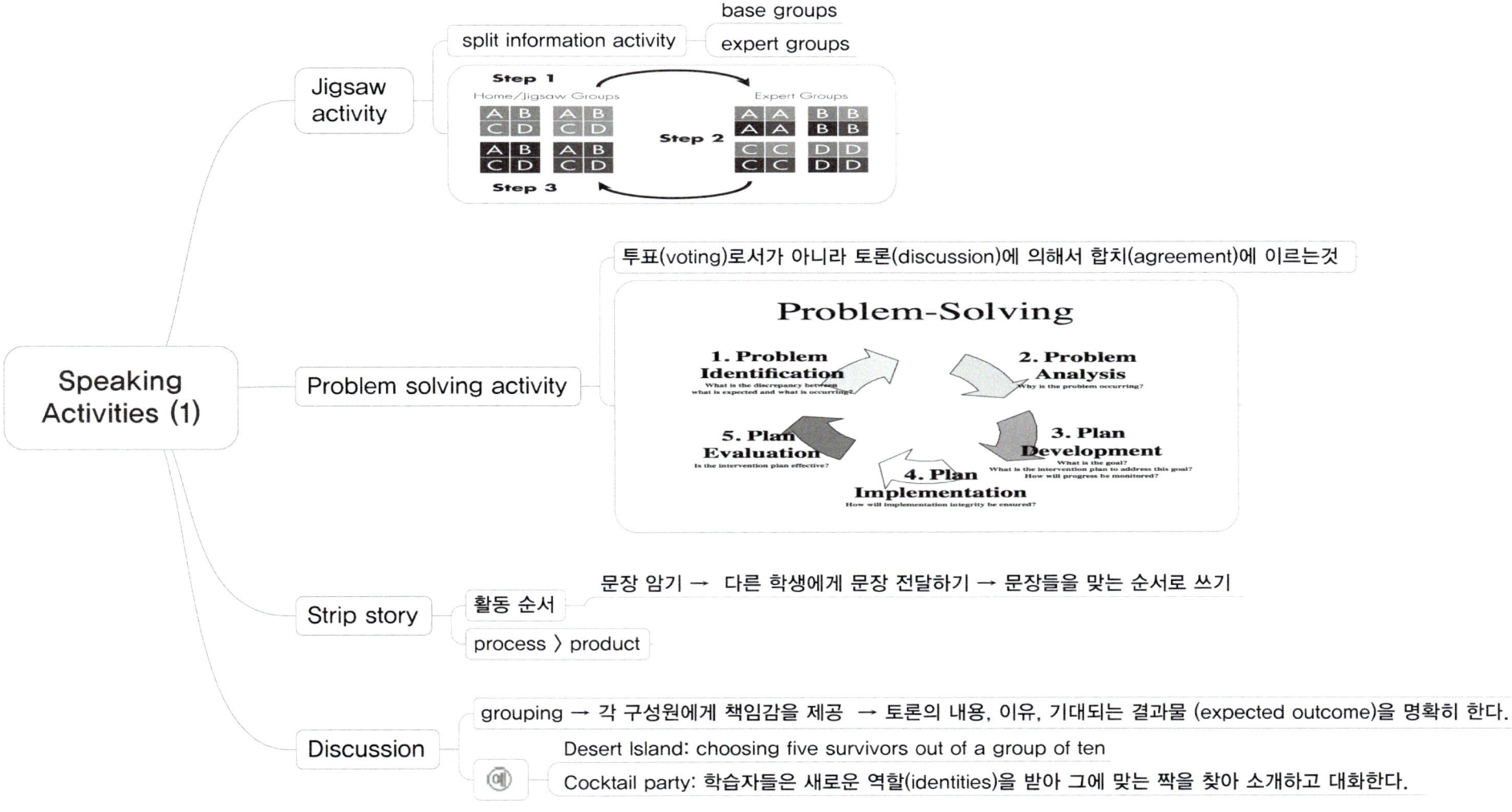

# 08 말하기 활동 (2)

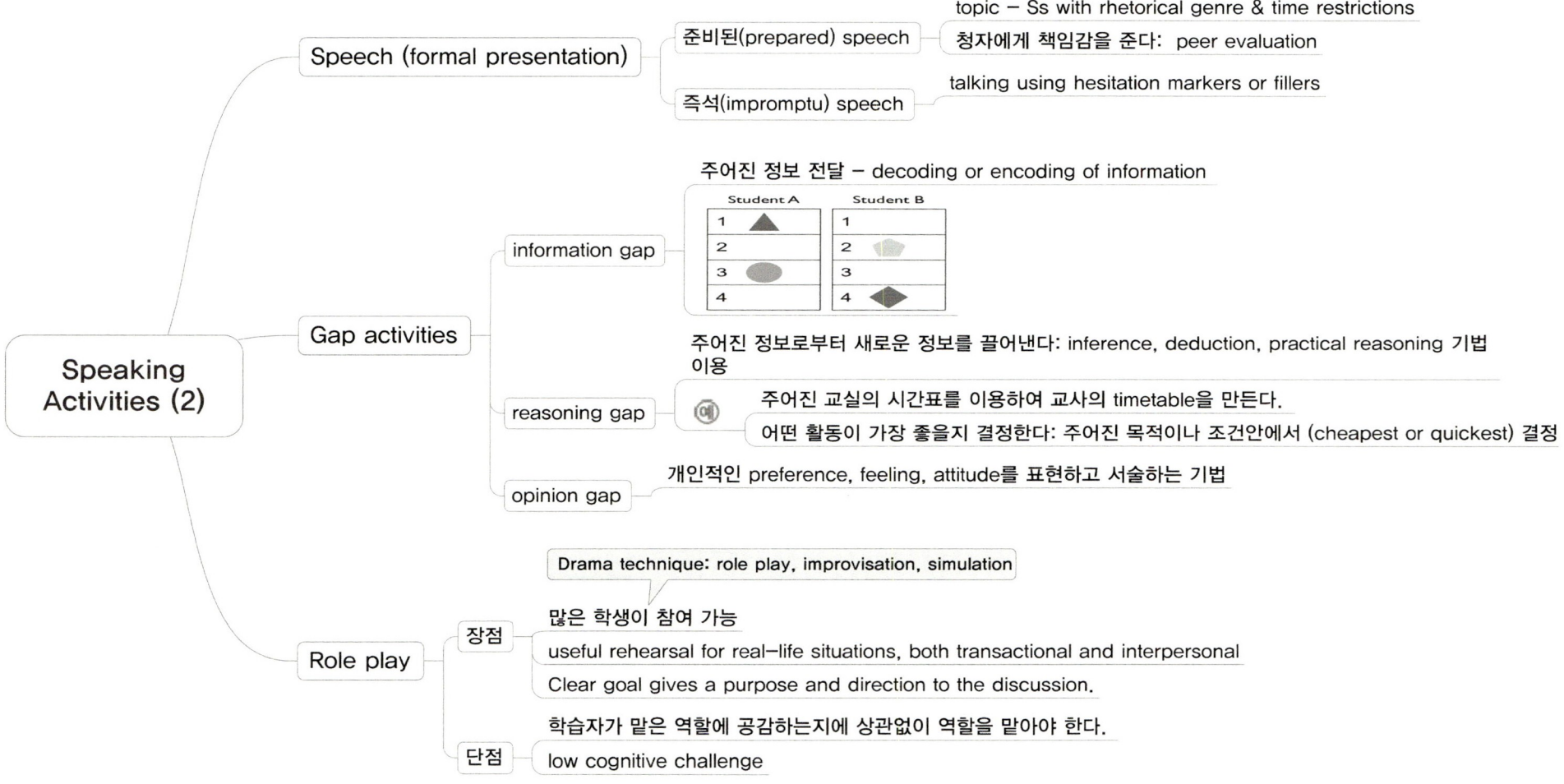

# 08.
# Teaching Reading

권영주 영어교육론 MIND MAP

# MEMO

권영주 영어교육론 MIND MAP

# 01 읽기 지도

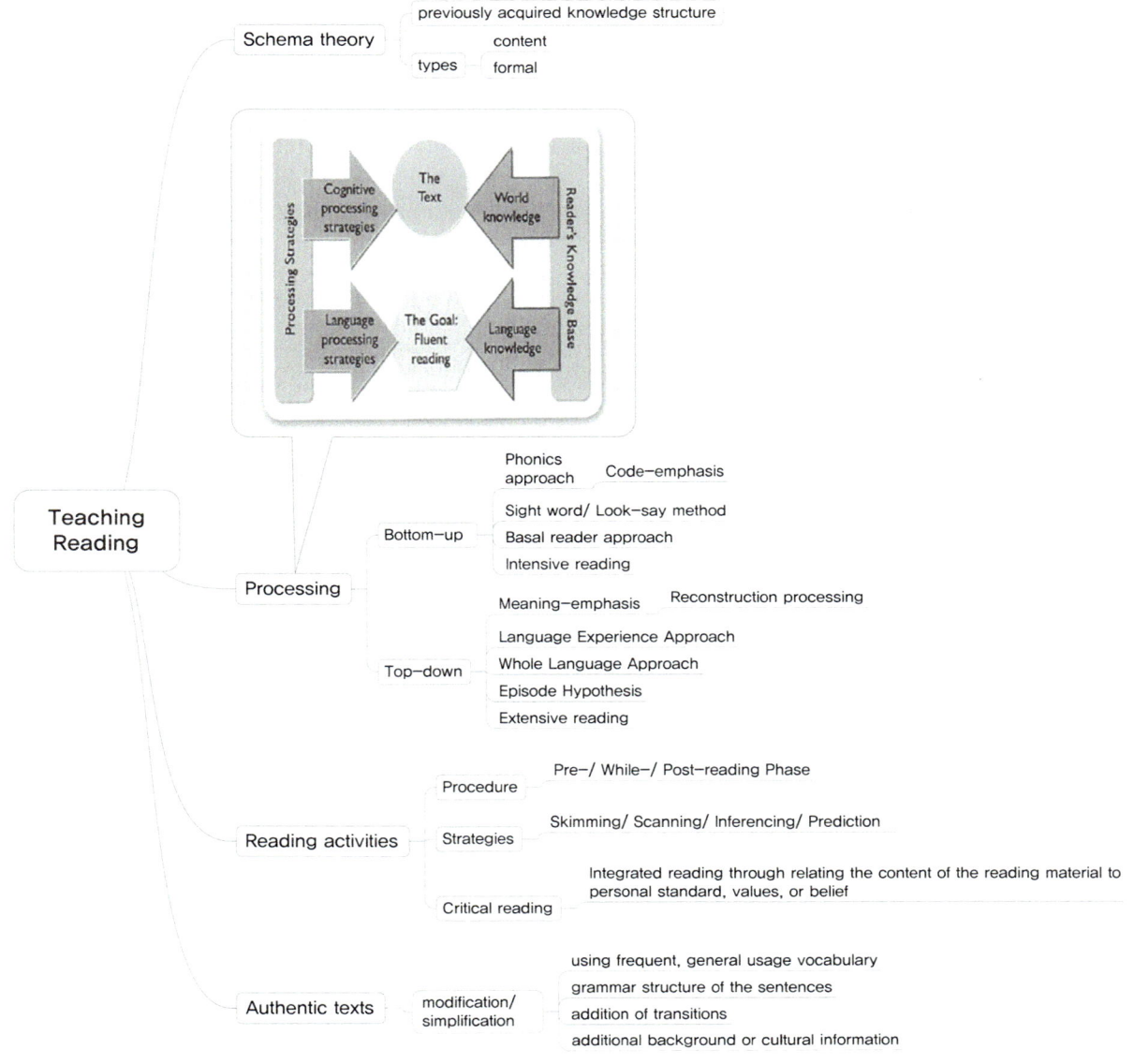

## 02 읽기수업 과정

**Reading Processing**

- **Top-down processing (Reconstruction)**
  - Whole language approach = meaning based approach + student centered
    - Individual readers choose what they want to read.
    - The reading is integrated with writing.
    - Emphasis is on constructing meaning.
    - (예) literature-based approach — authentic language and a wide range of vocabulary

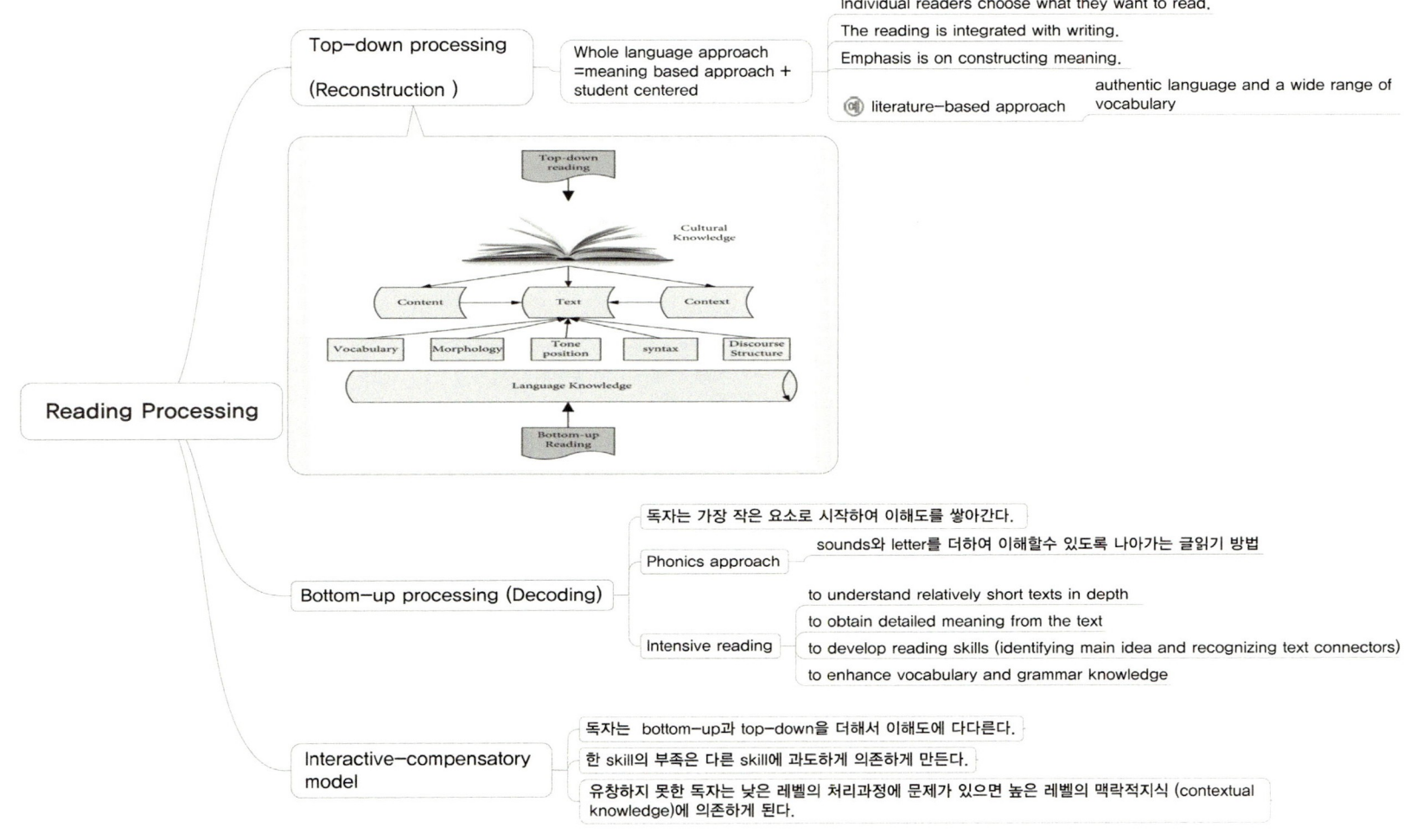

- **Bottom-up processing (Decoding)**
  - 독자는 가장 작은 요소로 시작하여 이해도를 쌓아간다.
  - Phonics approach — sounds와 letter를 더하여 이해할수 있도록 나아가는 글읽기 방법
  - Intensive reading
    - to understand relatively short texts in depth
    - to obtain detailed meaning from the text
    - to develop reading skills (identifying main idea and recognizing text connectors)
    - to enhance vocabulary and grammar knowledge

- **Interactive-compensatory model**
  - 독자는 bottom-up과 top-down을 더해서 이해도에 다다른다.
  - 한 skill의 부족은 다른 skill에 과도하게 의존하게 만든다.
  - 유창하지 못한 독자는 낮은 레벨의 처리과정에 문제가 있으면 높은 레벨의 맥락적지식 (contextual knowledge)에 의존하게 된다.

# 03 읽기 유형

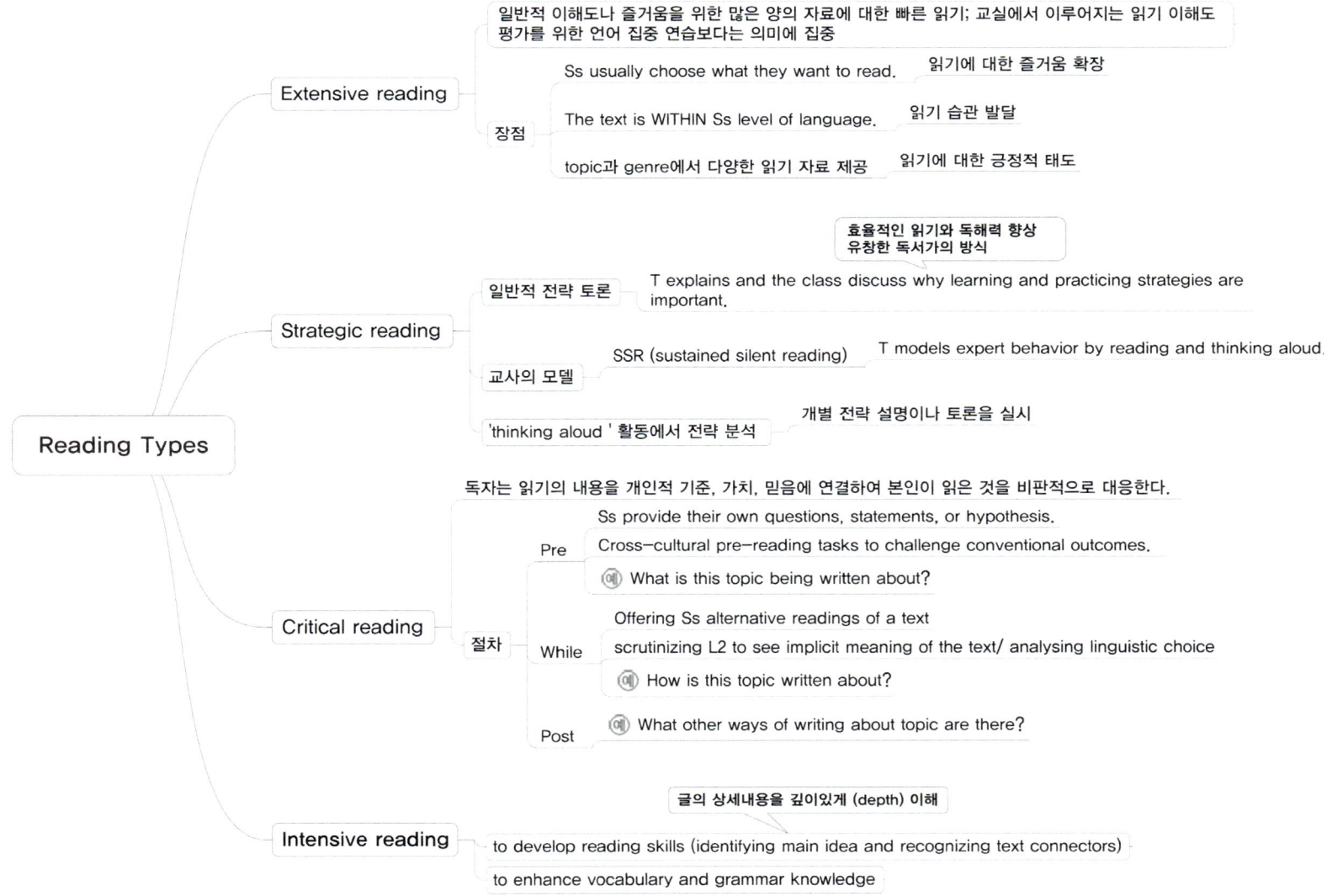

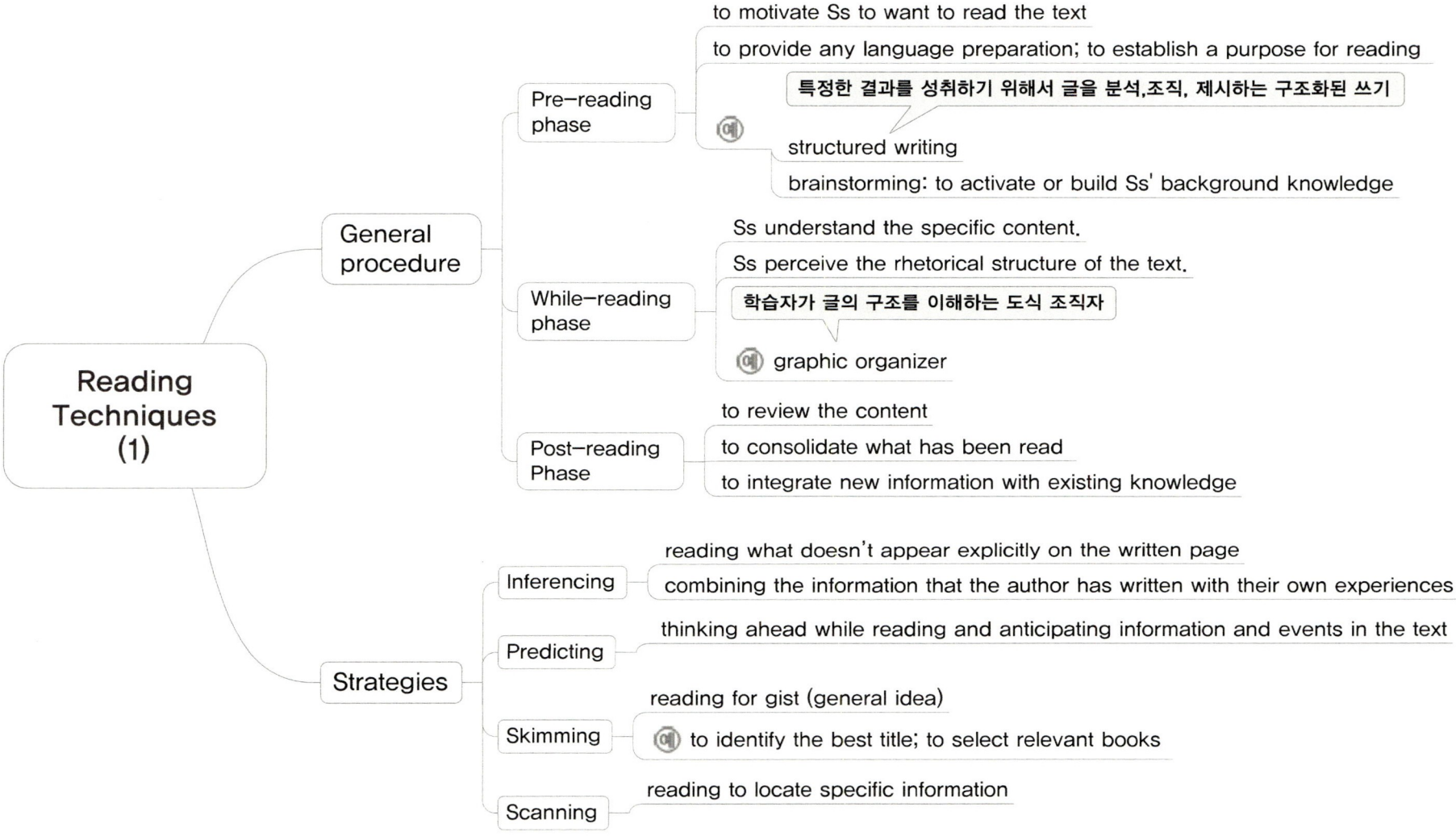

## 05 읽기 활동 방법 (2)

**MEMO**

# 09.
# Teaching Writing

권영주 영어교육론 MIND MAP

# MEMO

권영주 영어교육론 MIND MAP

# 01 쓰기 지도

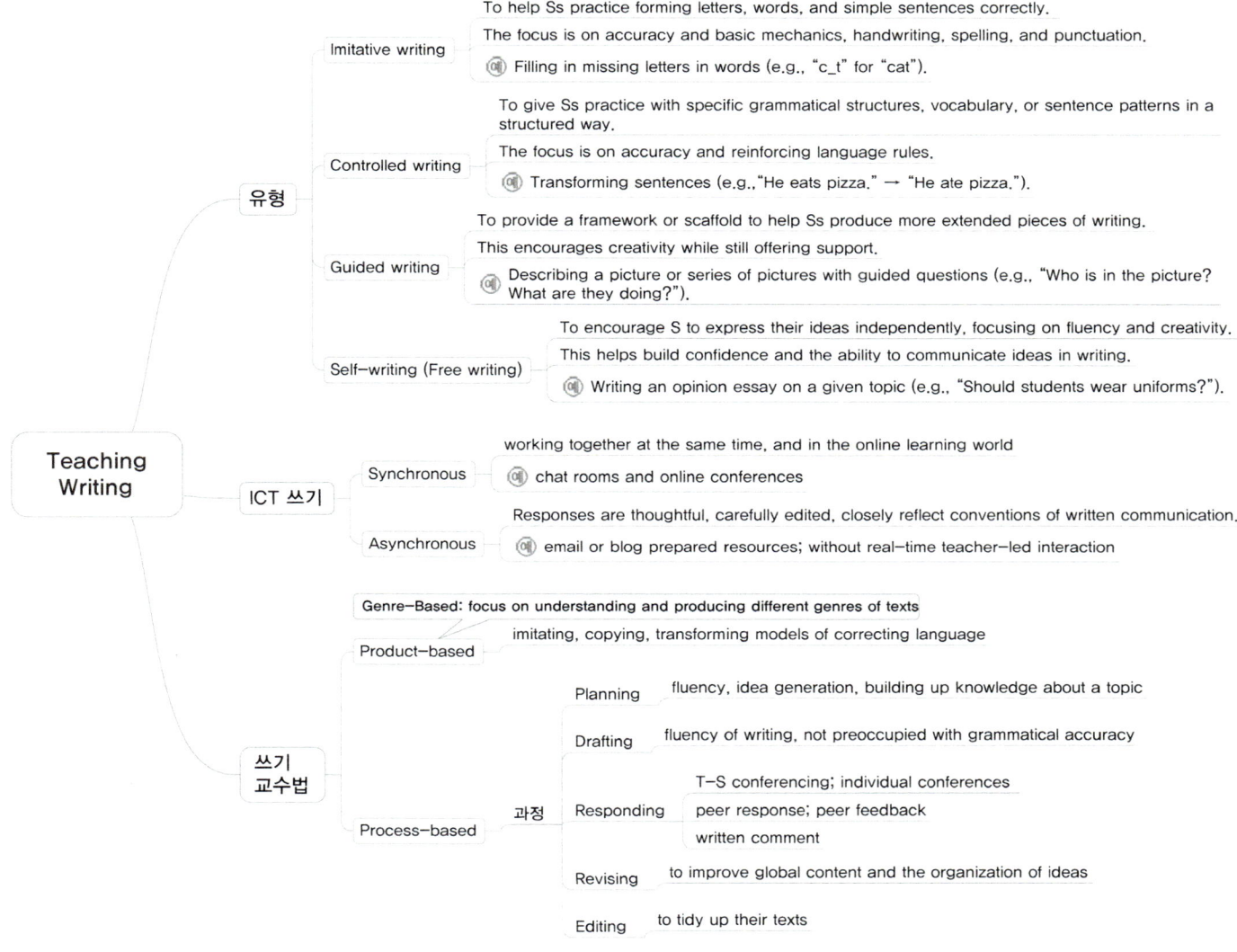

## 02 과정중심 쓰기 (1)

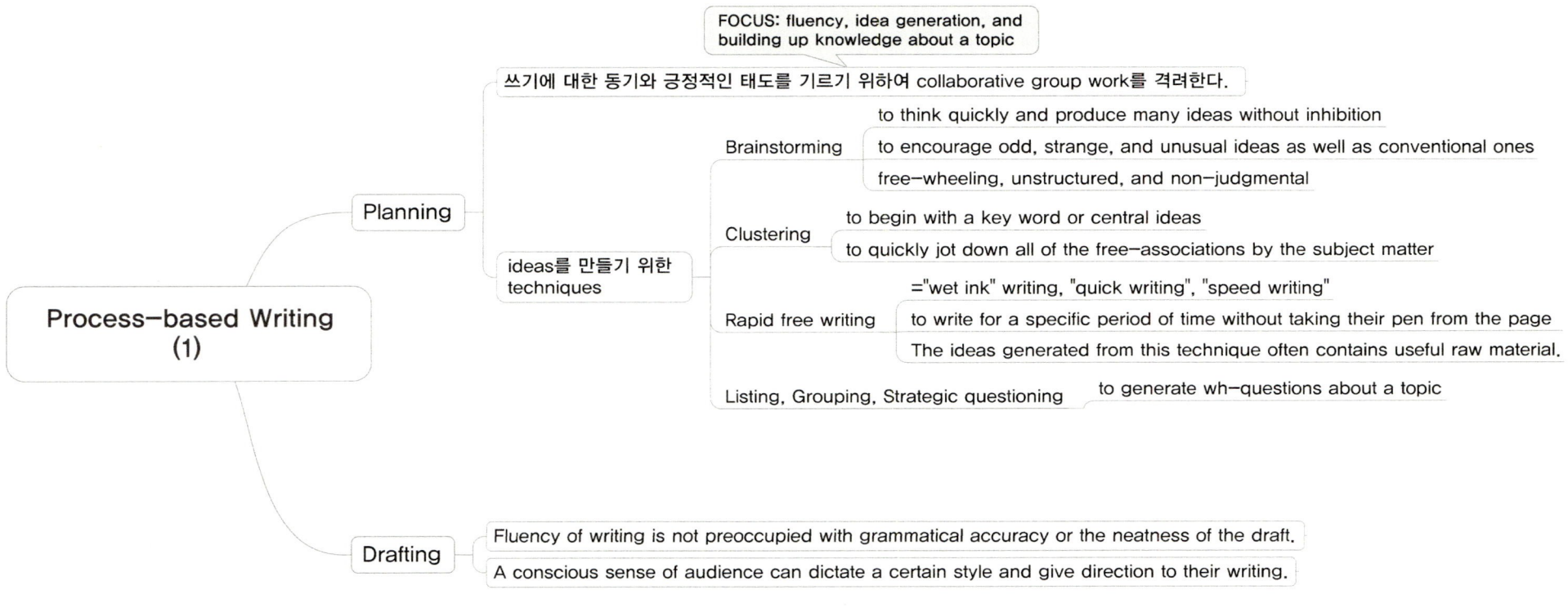

# 03 과정중심 쓰기 (2)

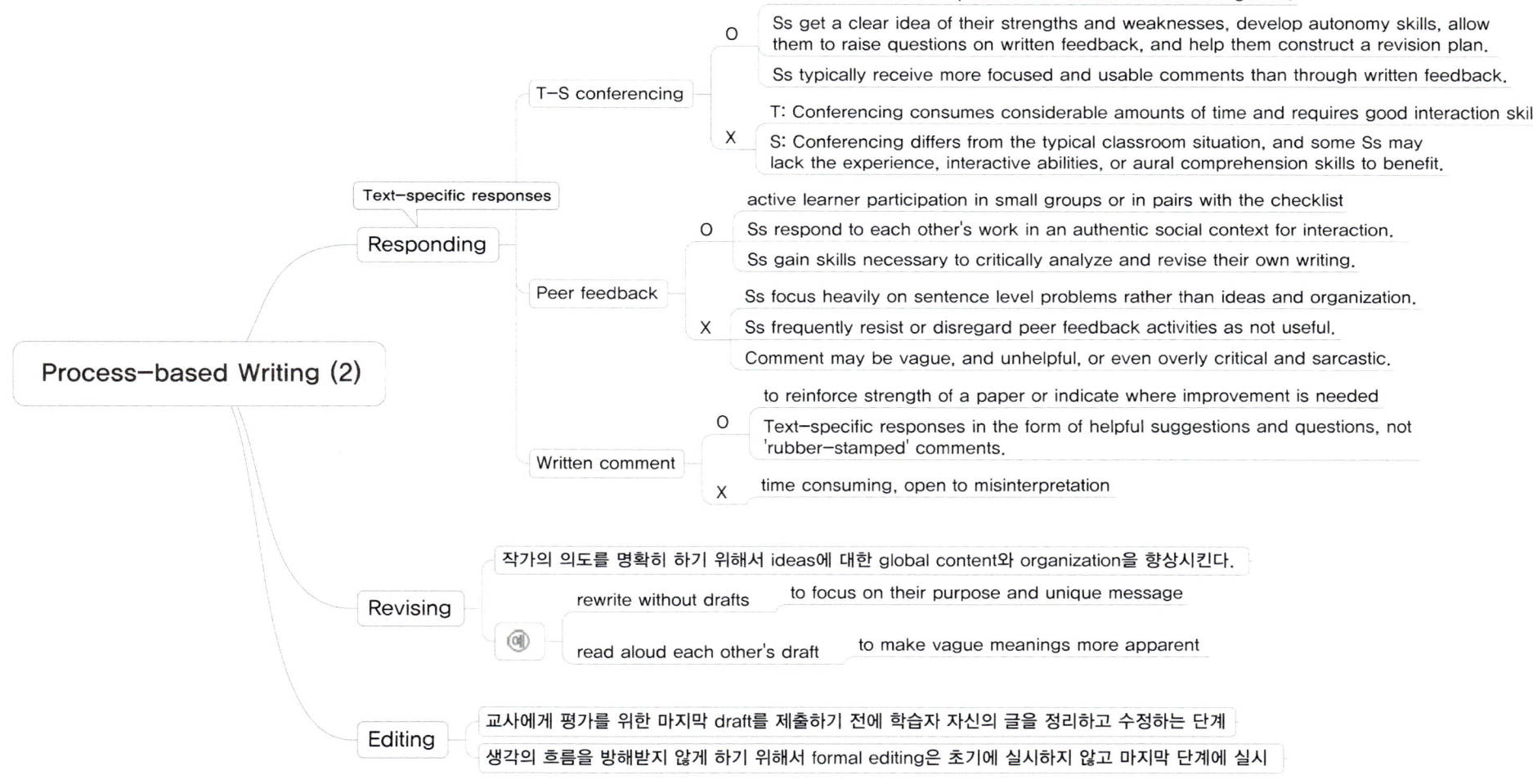

# 04 Genre중심 쓰기

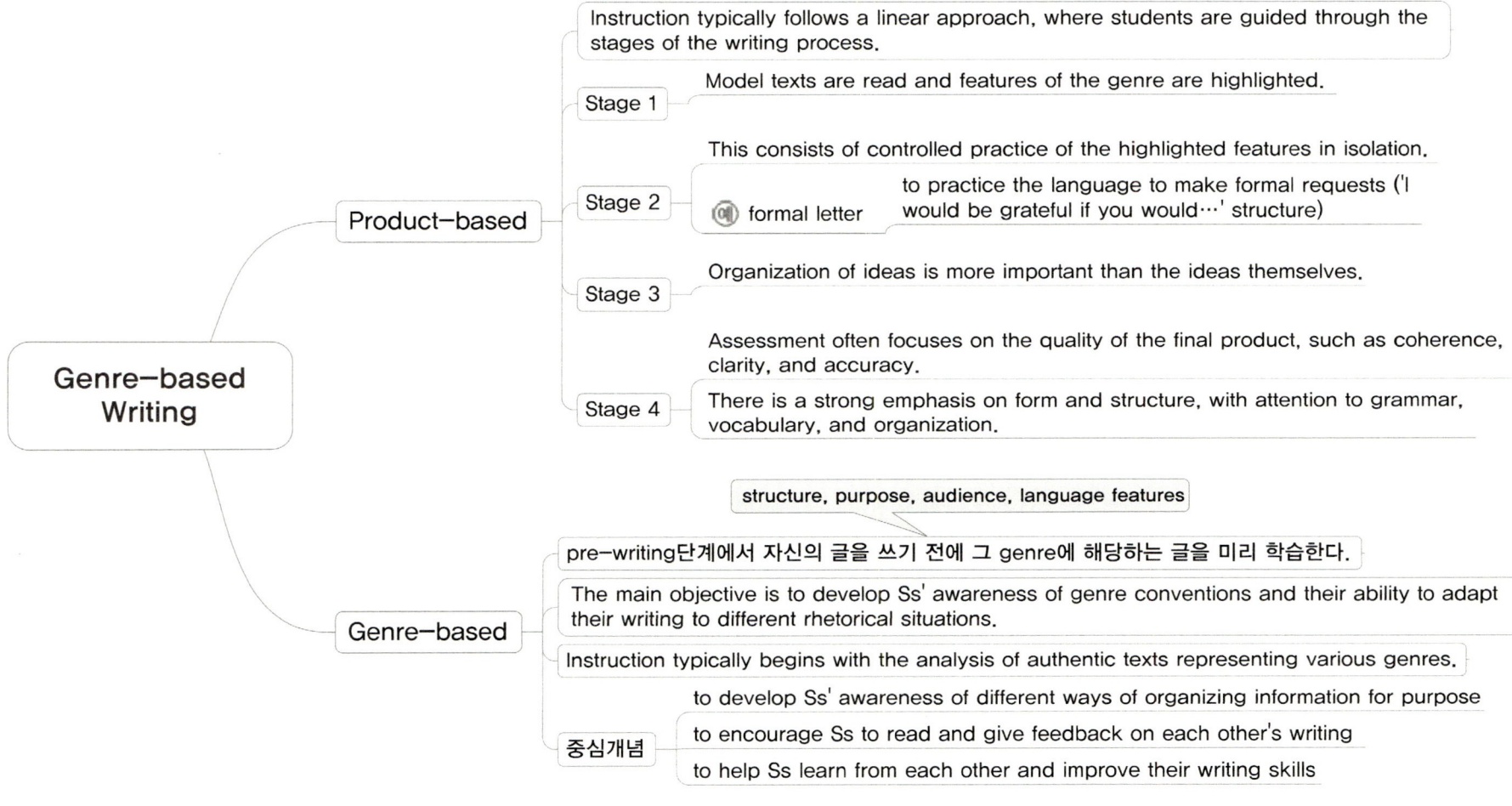

# 10.
# Teaching Grammar

권영주 영어교육론 MIND MAP

# MEMO

권영주 영어교육론 MIND MAP

# 01 문법 교실 수업

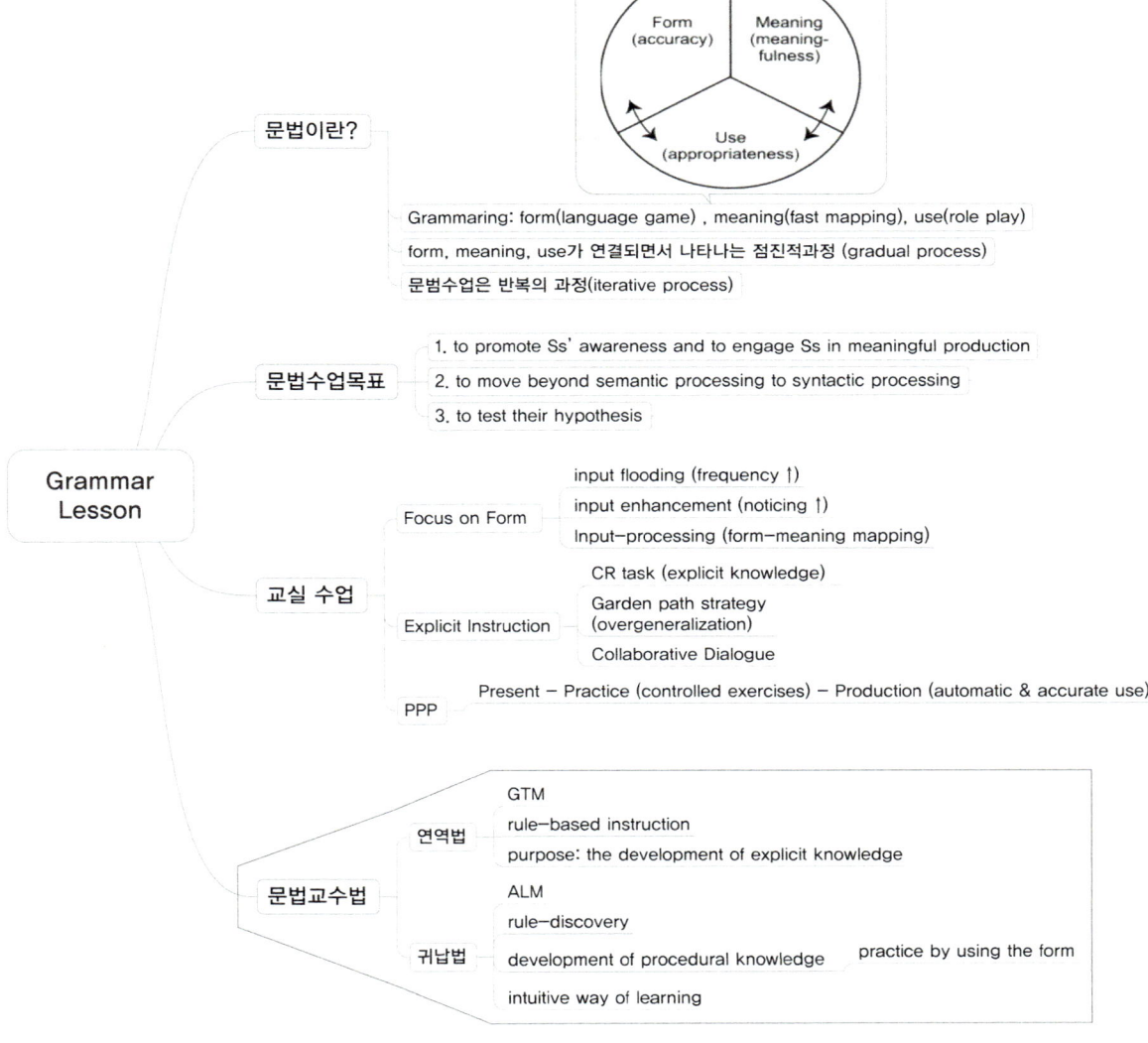

# 02 Focus on Form

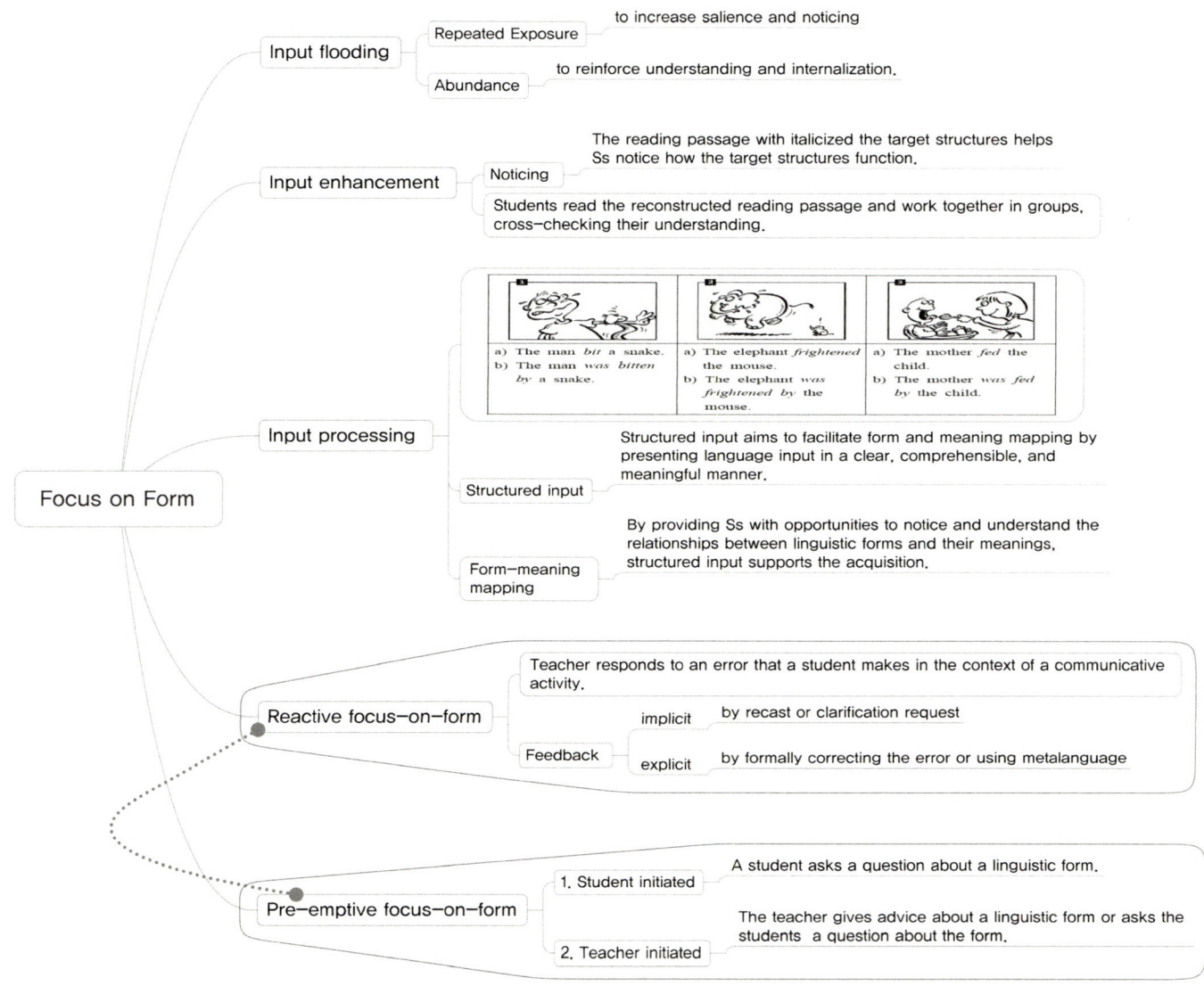

- **Focus on Form**
  - **Input flooding**
    - Repeated Exposure — to increase salience and noticing
    - Abundance — to reinforce understanding and internalization.
  - **Input enhancement**
    - Noticing — The reading passage with italicized the target structures helps Ss notice how the target structures function.
    - Students read the reconstructed reading passage and work together in groups, cross-checking their understanding.
  - **Input processing**
    - Structured input — Structured input aims to facilitate form and meaning mapping by presenting language input in a clear, comprehensible, and meaningful manner.
    - Form-meaning mapping — By providing Ss with opportunities to notice and understand the relationships between linguistic forms and their meanings, structured input supports the acquisition.
  - **Reactive focus-on-form**
    - Teacher responds to an error that a student makes in the context of a communicative activity.
    - Feedback
      - implicit — by recast or clarification request
      - explicit — by formally correcting the error or using metalanguage
  - **Pre-emptive focus-on-form**
    - 1. Student initiated — A student asks a question about a linguistic form.
    - 2. Teacher initiated — The teacher gives advice about a linguistic form or asks the students a question about the form.

# 03 명시적 문법수업

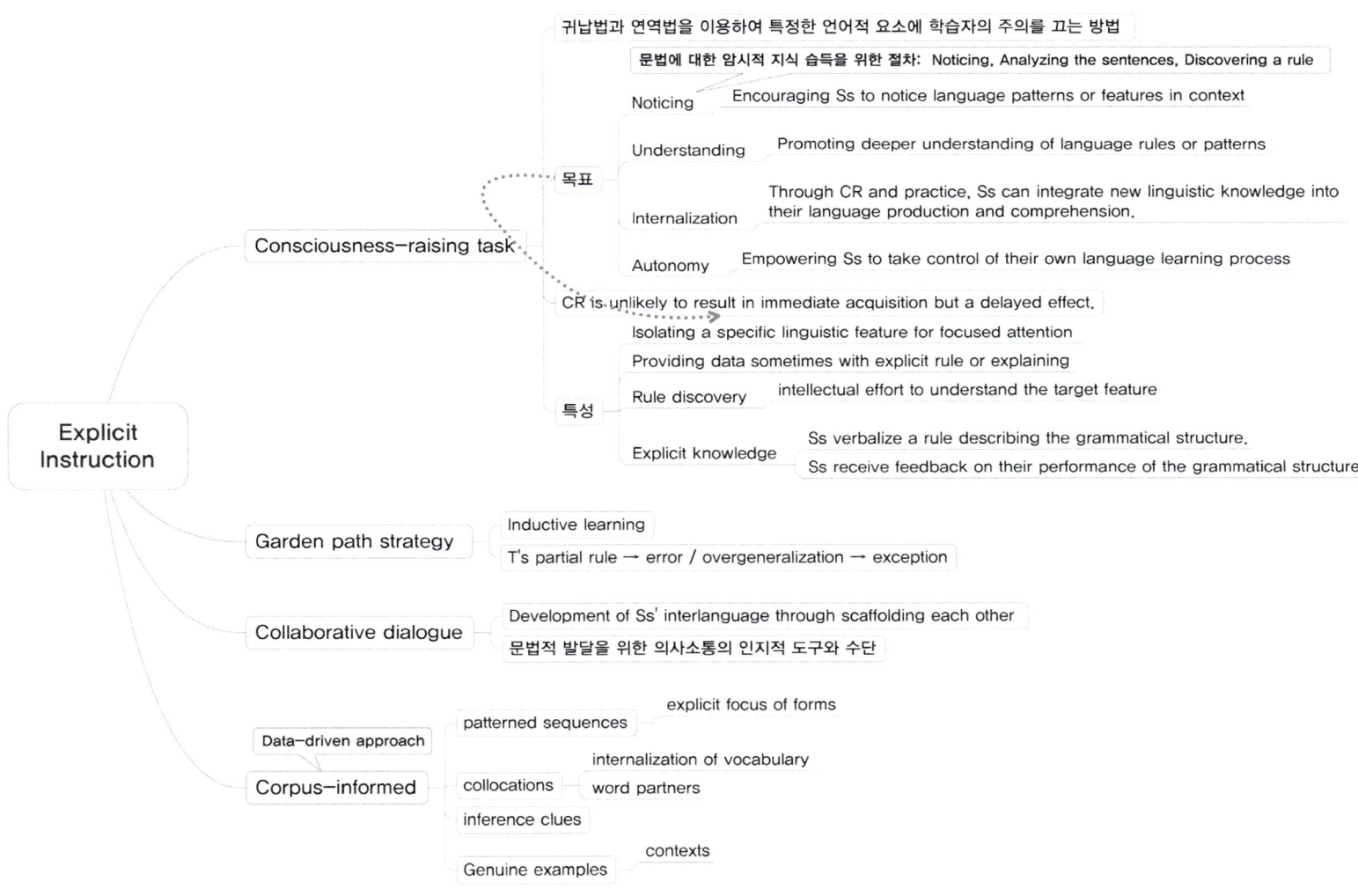

# 04 문법 교수법

## Focus on FormS 수업
- 구조적 교수요목 (structural syllabi)에 근거하여 문법을 가르치는 전통적 교수법
- 문법용어 (metalinguistic terms)를 사용하여 문법규칙 설명
- 문법을 정확하게 사용하게 하기 위해서 규칙의 이해도를 높이는 명시적 문법수업

## Grammar Teaching Approaches

**Deductive Approach**
Overtly explain the rule first. → Then provide specific examples to reinforce.

**Inductive Approach**
Provide specific examples first. → Then ask students to infer or deduce the rule.

### Deductive teaching
- 절차: Ss are taught rules and given specific information about a language.
- 문법규칙: Ss apply the rules when they use the language.
- 수업방법: Grammar translation method / study of the grammatical rules of a language

### Inductive teaching
- 절차: Ss are not taught grammatical or other types of rules directly but are left to discover or induce rules from their experience of using the language.
- 수업방법: Direct method, Communicative approach, and Counseling learning / to emphasize use of the language rather than presentation of information about the language

# 11. Teaching Vocabulary

권영주 영어교육론 MIND MAP

# MEMO

# 01 어휘 지도

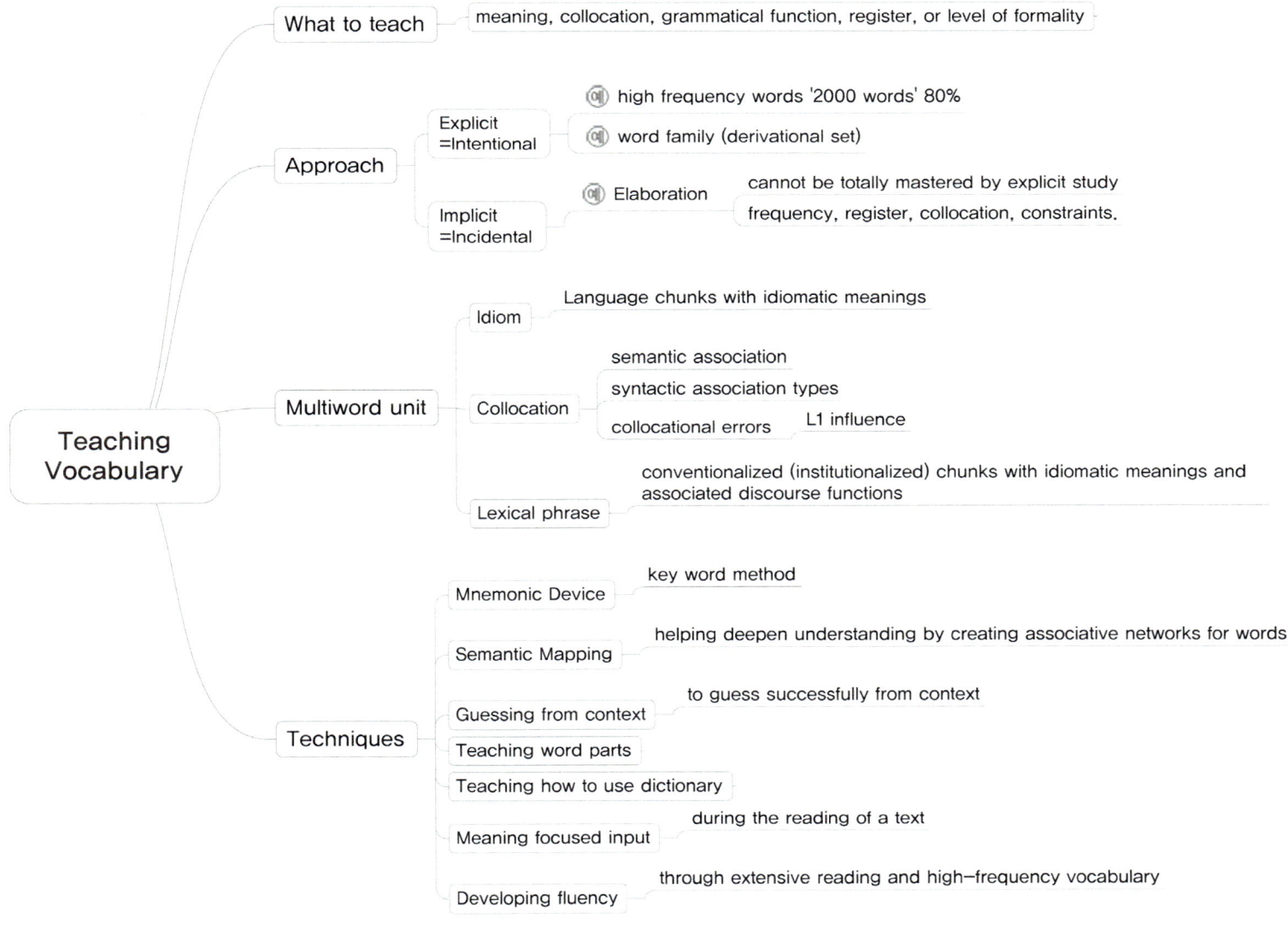

## 02 어휘 교수법

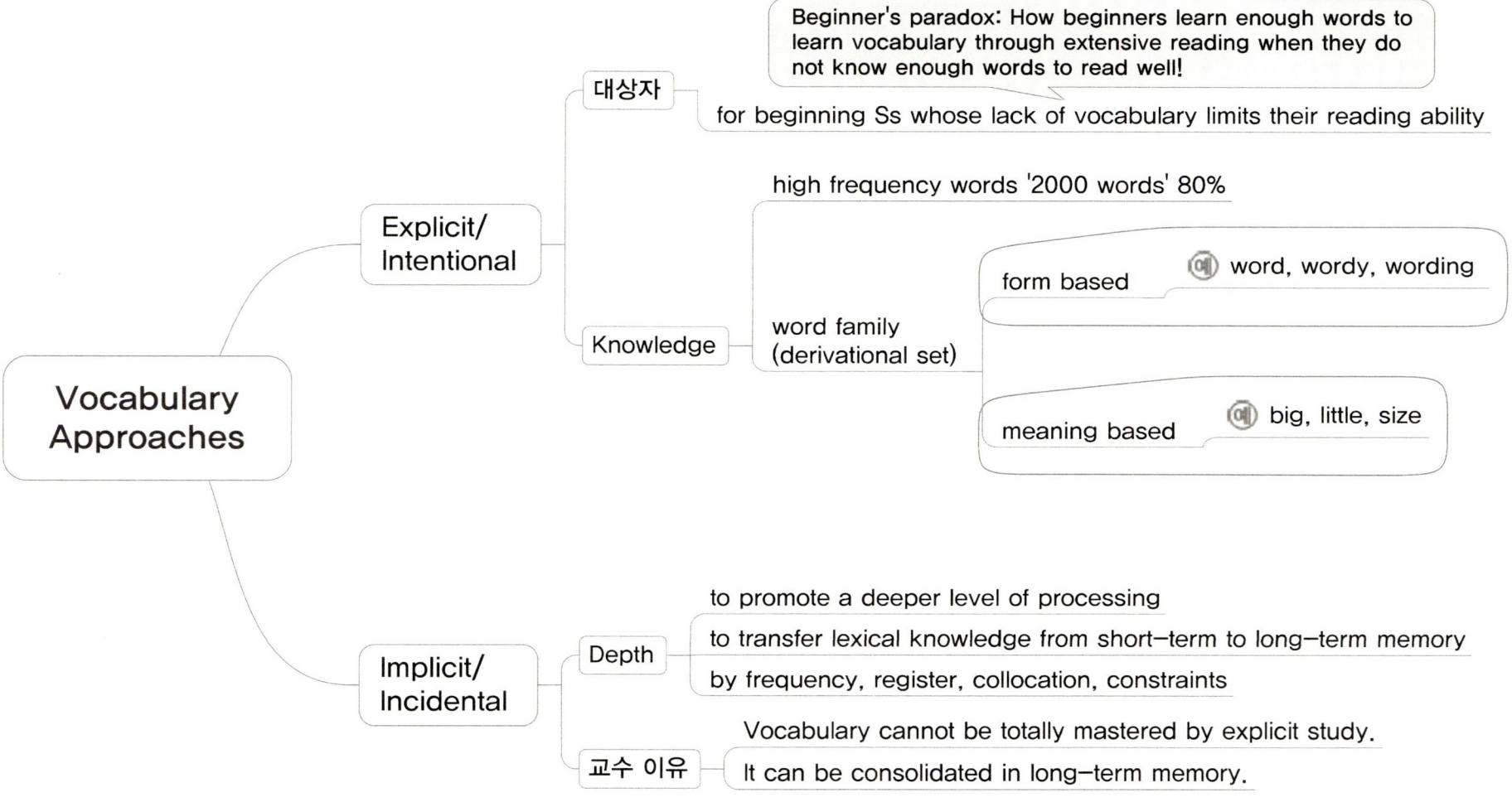

## 03 Lexis

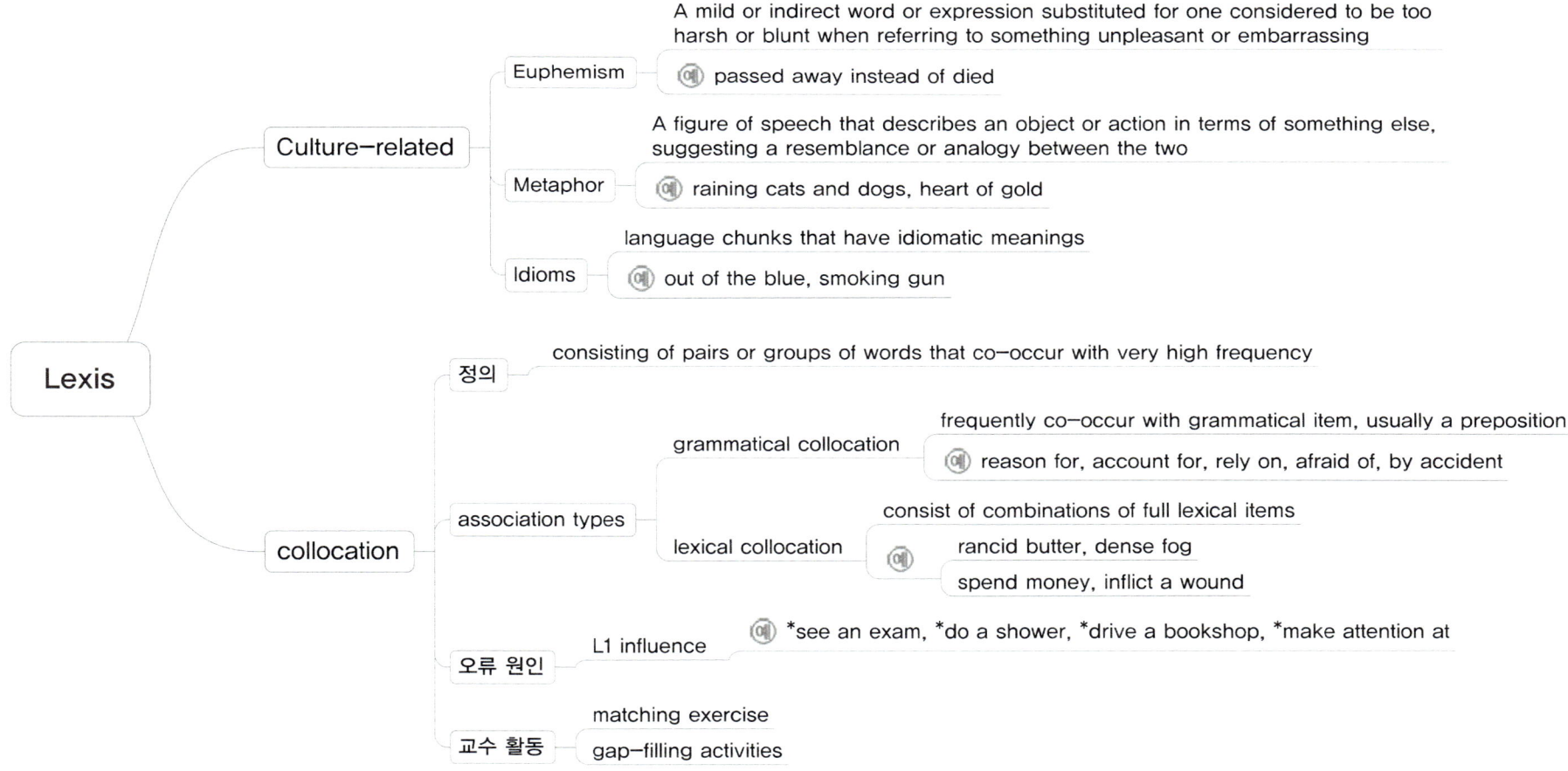

# 04 어휘 활동 방법 (1)

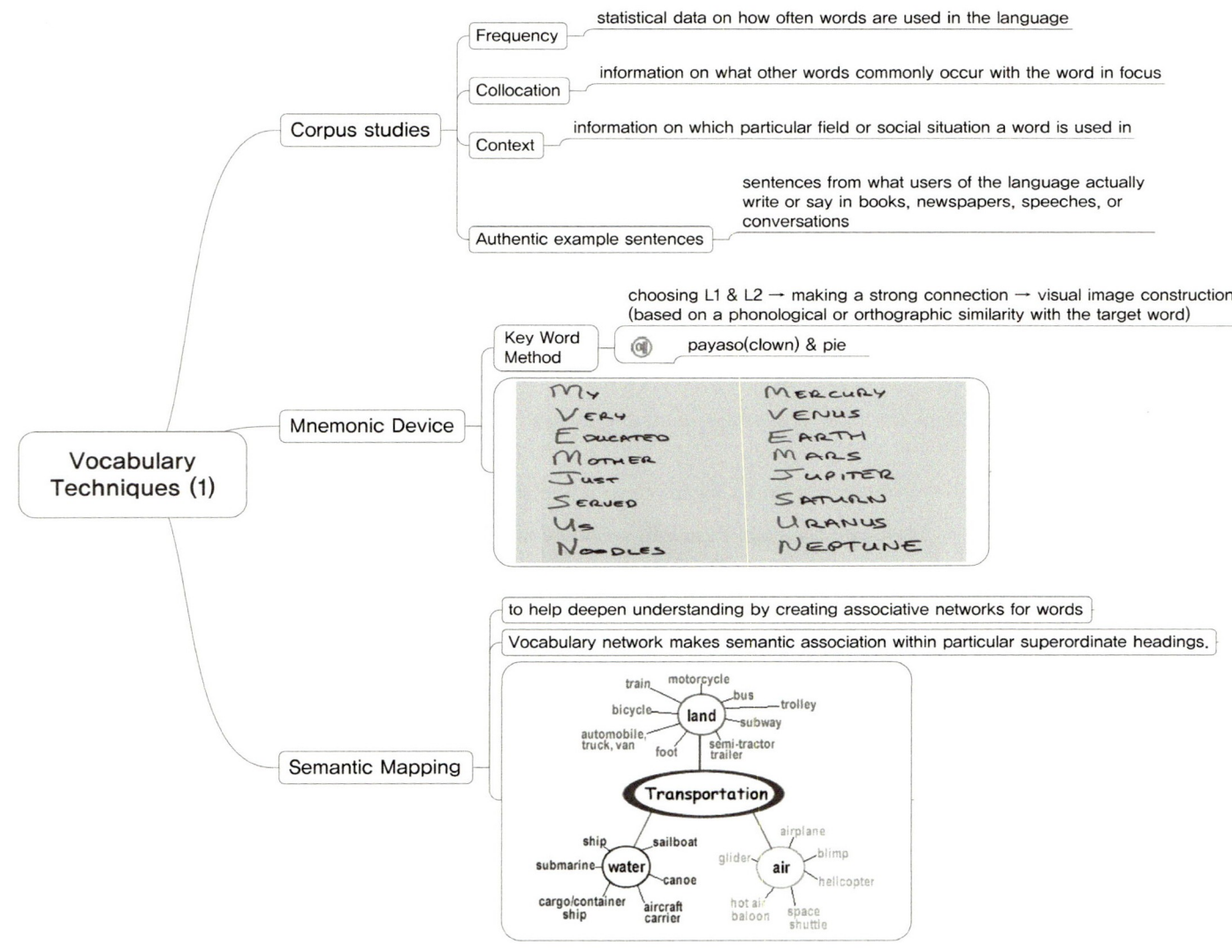

# 05 어휘 활동 방법 (2)

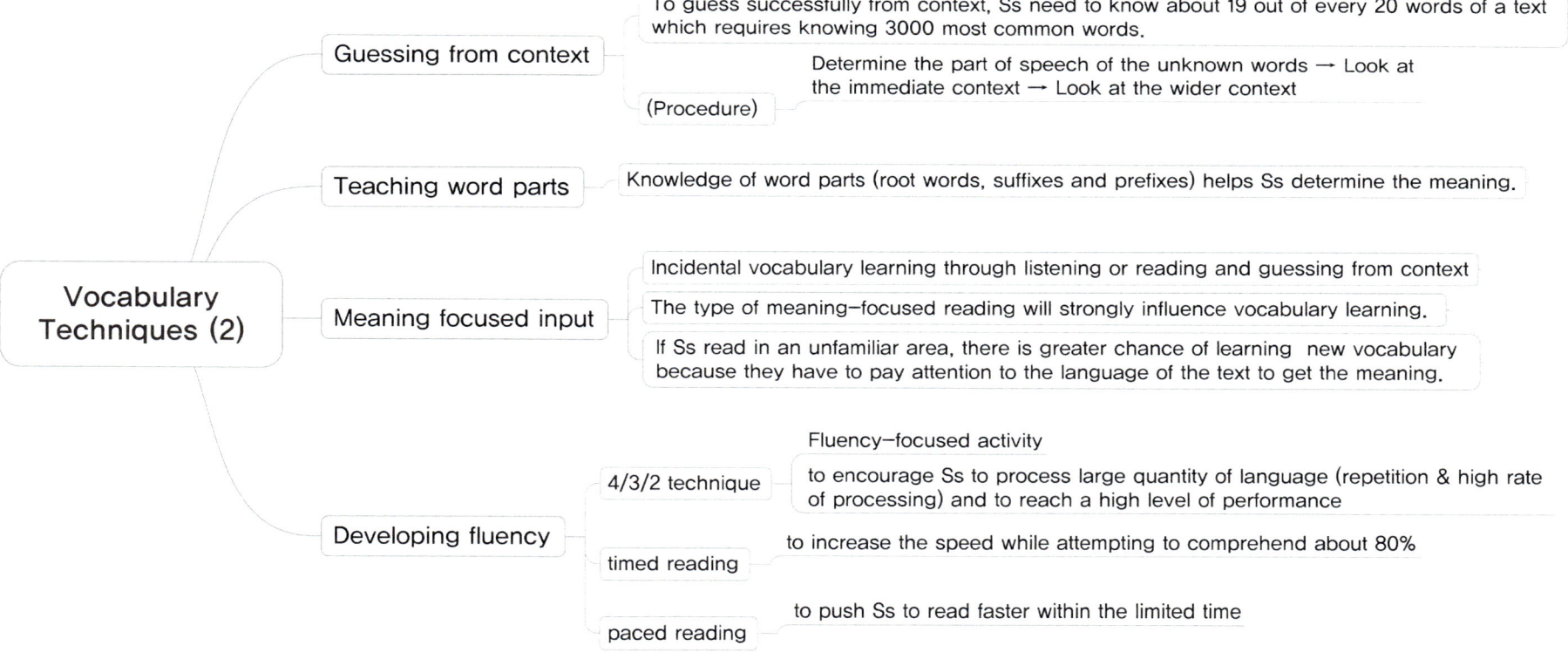

# 06 발음지도교수법

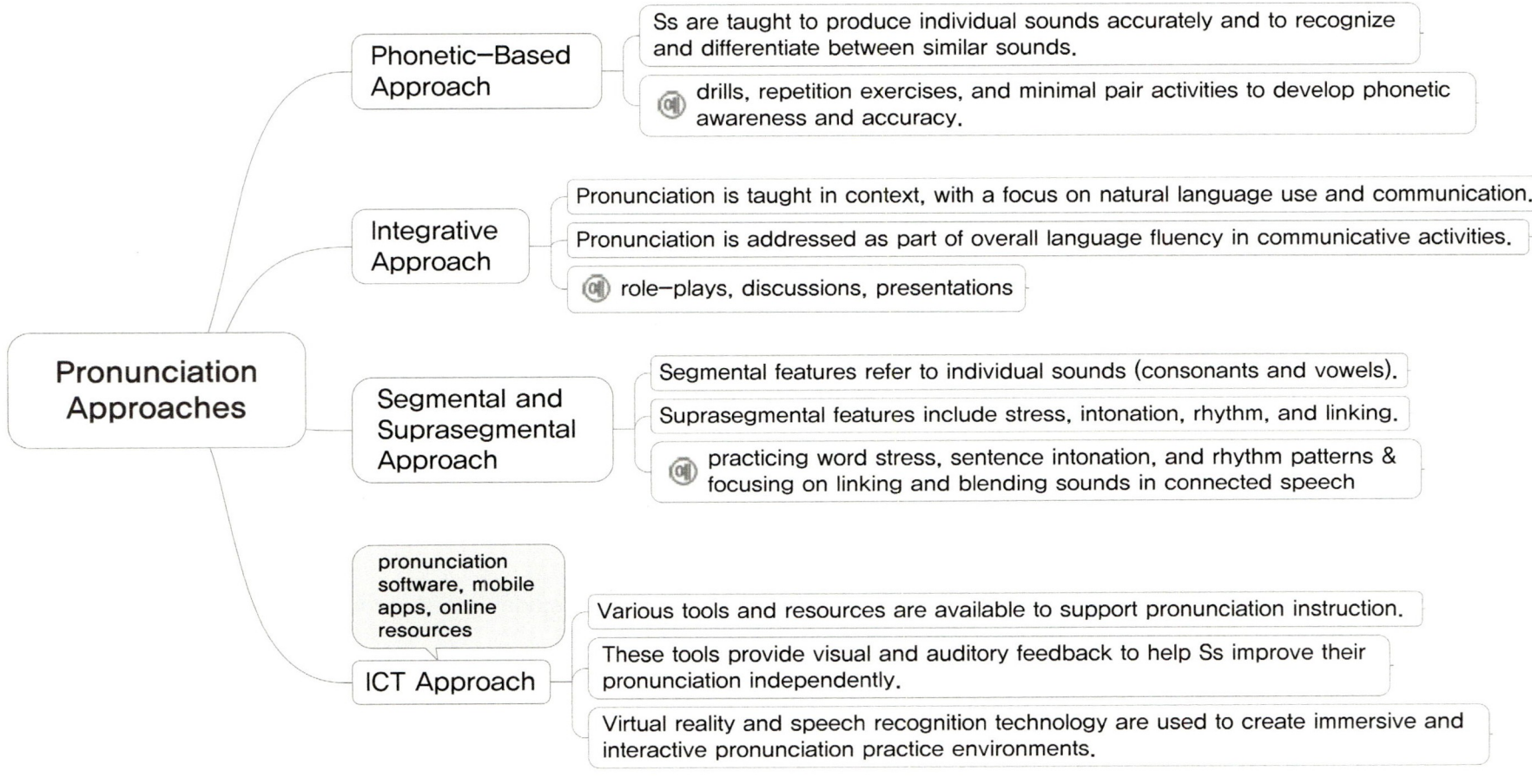

# 07 발음지도목표

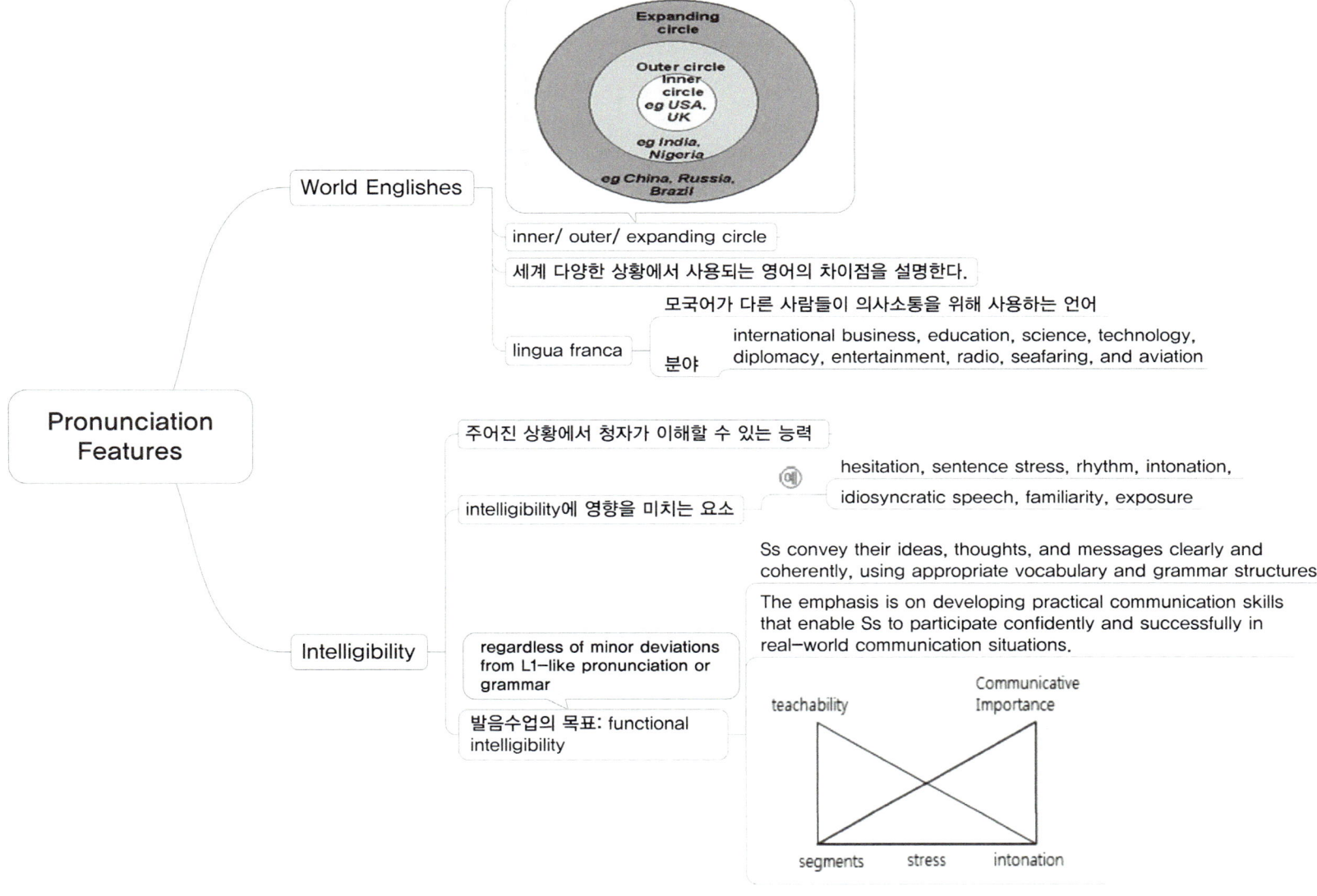

권영주 임용 전공

# 영어 교육론
## MIND MAP

**초판 1쇄 발행** 2023년 03월 02일
**개정 1쇄 발행** 2025년 02월 25일

**편저** 권영주
**발행인** 공태현  **발행처** (주)법률저널
**등록일자** 2008년 9월 26일  **등록번호** 제15-605호
**주소** 151-862 서울 관악구 복은4길 50 (서림동 120-32)
**대표전화** 02)874-1144  **팩스** 02)876-4312
**홈페이지** www.lec.co.kr
**ISBN** 978-89-6336-990-7 (13740)
**정가** 11,500원